HENRY VIII

·NO ·ÆTATIS· · SVÆ·XLIX

HENRY VIII

Frank Dwyer

CHELSEA HOUSE PUBLISHERS
NEW YORK
NEW HAVEN   PHILADELPHIA

EDITOR-IN-CHIEF: Nancy Toff
EXECUTIVE EDITOR: Remmel T. Nunn
MANAGING EDITOR: Karyn Gullen Browne
COPY CHIEF: Juliann Barbato
PICTURE EDITOR: Adrian G. Allen
ART DIRECTOR: Giannella Garrett
MANUFACTURING MANAGER: Gerald Levine

Staff for HENRY VIII:

SENIOR EDITOR: John W. Selfridge
ASSISTANT EDITORS: Sean Dolan, Kathleen McDermott
EDITORIAL ASSISTANT: James Guiry
COPY EDITORS: Gillian Bucky, Terrance Dolan, Michael Goodman, Ellen Scordato
ASSOCIATE PICTURE EDITOR: Juliette Dickstein
PICTURE RESEARCHER: Toby Greenberg
SENIOR DESIGNER: Ghila Krajzman
ASSISTANT DESIGNER: Jill Goldreyer
PRODUCTION COORDINATOR: Laura McCormick
COVER ILLUSTRATION: David Palladini

CREATIVE DIRECTOR: Harold Steinberg

Frontispiece courtesy of The Marsell Collection

First Printing

1 3 5 7 9 8 6 4 2

Library of Congress Cataloging in Publication Data

Dwyer, Frank. HENRY VIII

(World leaders past & present)
Bibliography: p.
Includes index.
1. Henry VIII, King of England, 1491–1547—Juvenile
literature. 2. Great Britain—Kings and rulers—Biography—
Juvenile literature. 3. Great Britain—History—Henry VIII,
1509–1547—Juvenile literature. [1. Henry VIII, King of
England, 1491–1547. 2. Kings, queens, rulers, etc. 3. Great
Britain—History—Henry VIII, 1509–1547]
I. Title. II. Series.
DA332.D99   1987   942.05'2'0924 [B] [92]   86-30981

ISBN 0-87754-530-8

Contents

ADENAUER	FREDERICK THE GREAT	MARY, QUEEN OF SCOTS
ALEXANDER THE GREAT	INDIRA GANDHI	GOLDA MEIR
MARC ANTONY	MOHANDAS GANDHI	METTERNICH
KING ARTHUR	GARIBALDI	MUSSOLINI
ATATÜRK	GENGHIS KHAN	NAPOLEON
ATTLEE	GLADSTONE	NASSER
BEGIN	GORBACHEV	NEHRU
BEN-GURION	HAMMARSKJÖLD	NERO
BISMARCK	HENRY VIII	NICHOLAS II
LÉON BLUM	HENRY OF NAVARRE	NIXON
BOLÍVAR	HINDENBURG	NKRUMAH
CESARE BORGIA	HITLER	PERICLES
BRANDT	HO CHI MINH	PERÓN
BREZHNEV	HUSSEIN	QADDAFI
CAESAR	IVAN THE TERRIBLE	ROBESPIERRE
CALVIN	ANDREW JACKSON	ELEANOR ROOSEVELT
CASTRO	JEFFERSON	FRANKLIN D. ROOSEVELT
CATHERINE THE GREAT	JOAN OF ARC	THEODORE ROOSEVELT
CHARLEMAGNE	POPE JOHN XXIII	SADAT
CHIANG KAI-SHEK	LYNDON JOHNSON	STALIN
CHURCHILL	JUÁREZ	SUN YAT-SEN
CLEMENCEAU	JOHN F. KENNEDY	TAMERLANE
CLEOPATRA	KENYATTA	THATCHER
CORTÉS	KHOMEINI	TITO
CROMWELL	KHRUSHCHEV	TROTSKY
DANTON	MARTIN LUTHER KING, JR.	TRUDEAU
DE GAULLE	KISSINGER	TRUMAN
DE VALERA	LENIN	VICTORIA
DISRAELI	LINCOLN	WASHINGTON
EISENHOWER	LLOYD GEORGE	WEIZMANN
ELEANOR OF AQUITAINE	LOUIS XIV	WOODROW WILSON
QUEEN ELIZABETH I	LUTHER	XERXES
FERDINAND AND ISABELLA	JUDAS MACCABEUS	ZHOU ENLAI
FRANCO	MAO ZEDONG	

ON LEADERSHIP
Arthur M. Schlesinger, jr.

LEADERSHIP, it may be said, is really what makes the world go round. Love no doubt smooths the passage; but love is a private transaction between consenting adults. Leadership is a public transaction with history. The idea of leadership affirms the capacity of individuals to move, inspire, and mobilize masses of people so that they act together in pursuit of an end. Sometimes leadership serves good purposes, sometimes bad; but whether the end is benign or evil, great leaders are those men and women who leave their personal stamp on history.

Now, the very concept of leadership implies the proposition that individuals can make a difference. This proposition has never been universally accepted. From classical times to the present day, eminent thinkers have regarded individuals as no more than the agents and pawns of larger forces, whether the gods and goddesses of the ancient world or, in the modern era, race, class, nation, the dialectic, the will of the people, the spirit of the times, history itself. Against such forces, the individual dwindles into insignificance.

So contends the thesis of historical determinism. Tolstoy's great novel *War and Peace* offers a famous statement of the case. Why, Tolstoy asked, did millions of men in the Napoleonic wars, denying their human feelings and their common sense, move back and forth across Europe slaughtering their fellows? "The war," Tolstoy answered, "was bound to happen simply because it was bound to happen." All prior history predetermined it. As for leaders, they, Tolstoy said, "are but the labels that serve to give a name to an end and, like labels, they have the least possible connection with the event." The greater the leader, "the more conspicuous the inevitability and the predestination of every act he commits." The leader, said Tolstoy, is "the slave of history."

Determinism takes many forms. Marxism is the determinism of class. Nazism the determinism of race. But the idea of men and women as the slaves of history runs athwart the deepest human instincts. Rigid determinism abolishes the idea of human freedom—

the assumption of free choice that underlies every move we make, every word we speak, every thought we think. It abolishes the idea of human responsibility, since it is manifestly unfair to reward or punish people for actions that are by definition beyond their control. No one can live consistently by any deterministic creed. The Marxist states prove this themselves by their extreme susceptibility to the cult of leadership.

More than that, history refutes the idea that individuals make no difference. In December 1931 a British politician crossing Park Avenue in New York City between 76th and 77th Streets around 10:30 P.M. looked in the wrong direction and was knocked down by an automobile—a moment, he later recalled, of a man aghast, a world aglare: "I do not understand why I was not broken like an eggshell or squashed like a gooseberry." Fourteen months later an American politician, sitting in an open car in Miami, Florida, was fired on by an assassin; the man beside him was hit. Those who believe that individuals make no difference to history might well ponder whether the next two decades would have been the same had Mario Constasino's car killed Winston Churchill in 1931 and Giuseppe Zangara's bullet killed Franklin Roosevelt in 1933. Suppose, in addition, that Adolf Hitler had been killed in the street fighting during the Munich *Putsch* of 1923 and that Lenin had died of typhus during World War I. What would the 20th century be like now?

For better or for worse, individuals do make a difference. "The notion that a people can run itself and its affairs anonymously," wrote the philosopher William James, "is now well known to be the silliest of absurdities. Mankind does nothing save through initiatives on the part of inventors, great or small, and imitation by the rest of us—these are the sole factors in human progress. Individuals of genius show the way, and set the patterns, which common people then adopt and follow."

Leadership, James suggests, means leadership in thought as well as in action. In the long run, leaders in thought may well make the greater difference to the world. But, as Woodrow Wilson once said, "Those only are leaders of men, in the general eye, who lead in action. . . . It is at their hands that new thought gets its translation into the crude language of deeds." Leaders in thought often invent in solitude and obscurity, leaving to later generations the tasks of imitation. Leaders in action—the leaders portrayed in this series—have to be effective in their own time.

And they cannot be effective by themselves. They must act in response to the rhythms of their age. Their genius must be adapted, in a phrase of William James's, "to the receptivities of the moment." Leaders are useless without followers. "There goes the mob," said the French politician hearing a clamor in the streets. "I am their leader. I must follow them." Great leaders turn the inchoate emotions of the mob to purposes of their own. They seize on the opportunities of their time, the hopes, fears, frustrations, crises, potentialities. They succeed when events have prepared the way for them, when the community is awaiting to be aroused, when they can provide the clarifying and organizing ideas. Leadership ignites the circuit between the individual and the mass and thereby alters history.

It may alter history for better or for worse. Leaders have been responsible for the most extravagant follies and most monstrous crimes that have beset suffering humanity. They have also been vital in such gains as humanity has made in individual freedom, religious and racial tolerance, social justice and respect for human rights.

There is no sure way to tell in advance who is going to lead for good and who for evil. But a glance at the gallery of men and women in *World Leaders—Past and Present* suggests some useful tests.

One test is this: do leaders lead by force or by persuasion? By command or by consent? Through most of history leadership was exercised by the divine right of authority. The duty of followers was to defer and to obey. "Theirs not to reason why,/ Theirs but to do and die." On occasion, as with the so-called "enlightened despots" of the 18th century in Europe, absolutist leadership was animated by humane purposes. More often, absolutism nourished the passion for domination, land, gold and conquest and resulted in tyranny.

The great revolution of modern times has been the revolution of equality. The idea that all people should be equal in their legal condition has undermined the old structure of authority, hierarchy and deference. The revolution of equality has had two contrary effects on the nature of leadership. For equality, as Alexis de Tocqueville pointed out in his great study *Democracy in America*, might mean equality in servitude as well as equality in freedom.

"I know of only two methods of establishing equality in the political world," Tocqueville wrote. "Rights must be given to every citizen, or none at all to anyone . . . save one, who is the master of all." There was no middle ground "between the sovereignty of all and the absolute power of one man." In his astonishing prediction of 20th-century totalitarian dictatorship, Tocqueville explained how the revolution of equality could lead to the "*Führerprinzip*" and more terrible absolutism than the world had ever known.

But when rights are given to every citizen and the sovereignty of all is established, the problem of leadership takes a new form, becomes more exacting than ever before. It is easy to issue commands and enforce them by the rope and the stake, the concentration camp and the *gulag*. It is much harder to use argument and achievement to overcome opposition and win consent. The Founding Fathers of the United States understood the difficulty. They believed that history had given them the opportunity to decide, as Alexander Hamilton wrote in the first Federalist Paper, whether men are indeed capable of basing government on "reflection and choice, or whether they are forever destined to depend . . . on accident and force."

Government by reflection and choice called for a new style of leadership and a new quality of followership. It required leaders to be responsive to popular concerns, and it required followers to be active and informed participants in the process. Democracy does not eliminate emotion from politics; sometimes it fosters demagoguery; but it is confident that, as the greatest of democratic leaders put it, you cannot fool all of the people all of the time. It measures leadership by results and retires those who overreach or falter or fail.

It is true that in the long run despots are measured by results too. But they can postpone the day of judgment, sometimes indefinitely, and in the meantime they can do infinite harm. It is also true that democracy is no guarantee of virtue and intelligence in government, for the voice of the people is not necessarily the voice of God. But democracy, by assuring the right of opposition, offers built-in resistance to the evils inherent in absolutism. As the theologian Reinhold Niebuhr summed it up, "Man's capacity for justice makes democracy possible, but man's inclination to injustice makes democracy necessary."

A second test for leadership is the end for which power is sought. When leaders have as their goal the supremacy of a master race or the promotion of totalitarian revolution or the acquisition and exploitation of colonies or the protection of greed and privilege or the preservation of personal power, it is likely that their leadership will do little to advance the cause of humanity. When their goal is the abolition of slavery, the liberation of women, the enlargement of opportunity for the poor and powerless, the extension of equal rights to racial minorities, the defense of the freedoms of expression and opposition, it is likely that their leadership will increase the sum of human liberty and welfare.

Leaders have done great harm to the world. They have also conferred great benefits. You will find both sorts in this series. Even "good" leaders must be regarded with a certain wariness. Leaders are not demigods; they put on their trousers one leg after another just like ordinary mortals. No leader is infallible, and every leader needs to be reminded of this at regular intervals. Irreverence irritates leaders but is their salvation. Unquestioning submission corrupts leaders and demands followers. Making a cult of a leader is always a mistake. Fortunately hero worship generates its own antidote. "Every hero," said Emerson, "becomes a bore at last."

The signal benefit the great leaders confer is to embolden the rest of us to live according to our own best selves, to be active, insistent, and resolute in affirming our own sense of things. For great leaders attest to the reality of human freedom against the supposed inevitabilities of history. And they attest to the wisdom and power that may lie within the most unlikely of us, which is why Abraham Lincoln remains the supreme example of great leadership. A great leader, said Emerson, exhibits new possibilities to all humanity. "We feed on genius. . . . Great men exist that there may be greater men."

Great leaders, in short, justify themselves by emancipating and empowering their followers. So humanity struggles to master its destiny, remembering with Alexis de Tocqueville: "It is true that around every man a fatal circle is traced beyond which he cannot pass; but within the wide verge of that circle he is powerful and free; as it is with man, so with communities."

1

Roses and Thorns

To the throne of England in 1509 came a young king of seemingly infinite promise, handsome and athletic, his life filled with laughter and music, with dancing and hunting and tilting with a lance in courtly tournaments, like one of the knights of King Arthur's time. Yet he later became so grossly fat and sick that he could barely be hoisted onto his horse. The young king married for love and rode, carrying his queen's colors, under the banner of "Sir Loyal Heart." Yet he put that queen aside and took a startling succession of new wives. He was a devout Catholic who wrote a book attacking the ideas of the German Protestant reformer Martin Luther, for which the pope gave him the grand title of "Defender of the Faith." Yet he would turn his back on that faith and declare himself supreme head of the church in England. He was a cunning and vigorous

conclusion!

He was . . . both the hero and the villain of the most dramatic reign in English history.
—WILL DURANT
American historian

Young Henry VIII, shown here at about the age of 20, was a king all England proudly and joyfully acclaimed. The great promise of his youth, however, would prove fleeting, and at the end of his long reign Henry was roundly detested.

Martin Luther posts his complaints against the Catholic church on a chapel in Wittenberg, Germany, 1517. Despite his early attacks on Lutheranism, Henry was to play an important role in the Protestant Reformation.

strategist, well-versed in international affairs. Yet he was constantly outsmarted and outmaneuvered by the kings, popes, and emperors of Europe. He was a shrewd judge of men and brought to power two ministers of such energy and capacity that they reformed both the royal court and the government and helped make England a modern state. They served him with single-minded devotion, yet he found reasons to destroy them both.

The story of Henry VIII might be said to begin about 80 years before his birth with another royal Henry, King Henry V. Henry V clothed himself in glory when he led his men to a famous victory near the French village of Agincourt on October 25, 1415. With most of France's nobility dead on the field, England's claims in France, including its claim to the French throne, seemed close to realization. Conquering France made Henry V extremely popular, and his popularity helped secure his claim to the English throne. He crowned his victory by marrying Catherine of Valois, the daughter of the king of France. The son of their union, another Henry, was expected to inherit the crowns of England and France. The people looked forward to a long reign for the hero-king and a smooth succession for his

King Henry V of England seeks the hand of the French princess Catherine of Valois. Henry's military exploits during the Hundred Years' War left a legacy that proved difficult for subsequent English kings, including Henry VIII, to live up to.

Henry VI, crowned in 1422, lost all his father's hard-fought territorial gains to France. His weakness as a ruler, periods of mental instability, and unpopularity led to challenges to his reign that culminated in the Wars of the Roses.

doubly royal son, but it was not to be. Henry V died in August 1422, in his 34th year, and during the reign of his son, King Henry VI, France reclaimed its independence.

Henry VI grew up to be a weak, indecisive king. His reign was marred by plotting and fighting between rival claimants to the throne. King Henry VI was the great-grandson of John of Gaunt, the duke of Lancaster, whose son, Henry, overthrew Richard II and took the English throne as Henry IV. His chief rivals were his cousins of the house of York. For 30 years, between 1455 and 1485, the English crown passed back and forth between the two warring houses. The Lancastrian faction adopted a red rose as its badge; the Yorkists a white. Their struggle is known as the Wars of the Roses. Five kings ruled England during the Wars of the Roses; three died violent deaths. Civil order broke down and outlawry flourished. The factionalism, the periodic shedding of noble blood, the misuse of power, and the dangerous disorder of Henry VI's early years came to seem almost the normal state of things. The very idea of kingship became less respected, identified with anarchy and conflict instead of law and order.

Some stability was achieved in the rule of the Yorkist King Edward IV, but he died young in 1483; his son became King Edward V at the age of 12. By that time no real Lancastrian threat to Yorkist rule existed, but Yorkist rivals dominated the young king. In July 1483 the boy's uncle stole the crown and made himself King Richard III. Edward and his brother disappeared mysteriously from the Tower of London, and their suspected murder caused widespread revulsion. An alliance was forged around an obscure relative of the king's, a provincial

The noble houses of York (represented by the white rose) and Lancaster (red rose) opposed each other from 1455 to 1485 for control of the English throne. Edward IV, son of Richard, duke of York, unseated Henry VI, the Lancastrian, in 1461.

Welshman named Henry Tudor, the earl of Richmond. This Henry could claim descent from the house of Lancaster on his mother's side, and a connection to the crown (albeit a less convincing one) on his father's side. Because the main line of the house of Lancaster had died out, the opponents of King Richard, if they wanted any color of legitimacy for their rebellion, had to back the slender claim of this little-known Welshman. Henry moved slyly to widen his support by contracting to marry Elizabeth of York, eldest daughter of the late King Edward IV and sister of the missing princes.

Any heirs of Henry and Elizabeth could claim to combine their father's red rose of Lancaster with their mother's white rose of York. If Henry Tudor could secure the crown and pass it on to a son, the long civil wars might finally come to an end. The blood of Lancaster and York would no longer be so regularly spilled if it could be mingled in a Tudor child.

Supported by French ships, troops, and money, Henry Tudor landed at Milford Haven in western Wales in August 1485, crossed quickly into England, and engaged the forces of King Richard at Bosworth Field, where the desperate, despised Richard lost both his crown and his life.

Henry Tudor would rule England as Henry VII. He soon married Elizabeth of York, and their first child, a son, was born not quite nine months after the wedding. Even the christening of the eagerly awaited heir proved to be an important matter of Tudor statecraft. The infant prince was named Ar-

Henry VII knew how fortunate he was to be on the throne of England, and how lucky he would be if he stayed there.
—ROBERT LACEY
British historian

Richard III loses his life at Bosworth Field in August 1485. His defeat signaled the end of the Wars of the Roses and Yorkist rule in England.

thur, after the beloved king of British legend. Any Englishman, superstitious or not, might pause before joining a rebellion against a king with such a powerful, magical name.

There was no comparable magic in the name Henry. Every king in living memory had been preoccupied with the threat of rebellion by rival claimants to the crown backed by the Scots or the Irish or the French. All through his 24-year reign, Henry VII would be plagued by these pretenders and their ambitious supporters.

The king met each challenge swiftly and firmly, laboring to restore the rule of law, to nourish peace, and to secure the Tudor crown that would guarantee both. Though various pretenders to the throne arose, the English people shared the king's desire for peace, as the alternative was the anarchy and strife that accompanied dynastic struggles. Once, after a similar period of anarchy and disorder, an enlightened king named Arthur had appeared to bring England a blessed time of prosperity, justice, and peace. The people could hope that a Tudor Arthur would bring another Camelot. They would be willing to accept, ignore, and forgive many things in exchange for the benefits of a strong rule. For his part, King Henry VII worked diligently to leave a secure throne and a stable nation for his well-named prince.

Given the ordinary hazards of 15th-century life and the political risk of having only one possible successor, no king would be satisfied with just one son. Queen Elizabeth bore eight children from the birth of Arthur in 1486 to her early death in childbirth in 1503. Of the eight, only four were sons, and two of them died in infancy, so only two of the eight children could realistically be regarded as heirs. (To this point, no woman had ruled as England's monarch.) The elder son, the heir apparent, was Arthur, Prince of Wales. The younger son was Arthur's rambunctious younger brother, another royal Henry.

In 1485 Henry Tudor, a Welsh Lancastrian, defeated Richard III at the Battle of Bosworth Field. Although a relative unknown, Henry VII proved to be an effective, if not very popular, leader.

King Henry VII married Elizabeth of York in 1486, uniting the warring houses in the hope of permanently ending their feud.

2

The Dancing Prince

Prince Henry was born at the Greenwich Palace, London, on June 28, 1491. As the king's second son, he received many honors and titles. In his first known official act five-year-old Prince Henry witnessed the granting of a royal charter to the abbey and convent of Glastonbury giving them permission to hold two fairs every year. In later life, however, he would not be a very good friend to the monks and nuns of Glastonbury. There is even more irony in another glimpse we have of his early years. On November 14, 1501, all London gathered to watch as the red-haired 10-year-old, bursting with vitality and solemn importance, led the procession bringing Catherine of Aragon, the 15-year-old daughter of King Ferdinand of Spain, to St. Paul's Cathedral for her wedding with his brother, Arthur. Before long Henry would lead Catherine to another church and marry her himself.

Already [there was] something of royalty in his demeanor . . . a certain dignity combined with a singular courtesy.
—ERASMUS
Dutch philosopher, on eight year-old Prince Henry

Henry was a well-read young man whose intelligence and interest in the arts, history, and theology impressed the noted scholars Erasmus and Thomas More. He absorbed from his tutors a deep skeptical secularism that would later have profound consequences.

In marked contrast to his elder brother, Arthur, Henry (shown here as an infant) grew to be a carefree, fun-loving youth who impressed the court with his eager curiosity and hearty spirit.

There is nothing wanting in her that the most beautiful girl should have.

—THOMAS MORE
English statesman and scholar on Catherine of Aragon, 1501

The union of Arthur and Catherine crowned an alliance between their fathers, the kings of England and Spain, against their common enemy, the powerful King Louis XII of France. The marriage was a diplomatic masterstroke for Henry VII, and it dazzled his subjects, who had not seen England play much of a part in the great world beyond her island shores since the glory days of Henry V. It also made a powerful impression on every court in Europe. King Henry was a provincial whose attention was necessarily focused on domestic problems, but his beautiful and accomplished daughter-in-law would doubtless be queen of a much more sophisticated, cultivated, and outward-looking court. When the prince and princess produced an heir, and the Tudor crown and succession were secure, England could think of playing a larger role in the destiny of Europe.

Catherine of Aragon was singularly well-suited to make these dreams come true. She was bright, gracious, animated, devout, and very well educated, a product of the new learning of the Renaissance. Spain had welcomed the sudden flourishing of philosophy, poetry, and art that began in 14th-century Italy. Catherine and her retinue brought to England a strong current of Renaissance excitement.

They brought other, darker currents as well, some in clear conflict with the freedom and openness of the Renaissance. Catherine was a child of two extraordinary parents, a couple whose marriage had united and revitalized Spain. Her father, who ruled the eastern portion of Spain known as Aragon, was a typical medieval king in some respects, happiest when he was out hunting or hawking or making war, but he also displayed great cunning and single-mindedness in securing and extending his power. Catherine's mother, Isabella of Castile, the western portion of Spain, was a deeply pious warrior-queen who managed to encourage both the new light of the Renaissance and the old darkness of religious persecution and terror, as symbolized by the infamous Inquisition. The Spanish Inquisition was a council established to root out and punish heretics — those who did not conform to the beliefs and prac-

Catherine of Aragon was the youngest daughter of the Spanish monarchs Ferdinand and Isabella. A highly intelligent and very devout woman, Catherine was wed to Arthur Tudor in November 1501; not five months later she was left a widow.

tices of Roman Catholicism. It became, however, a royal instrument used to persecute any religious, political, or cultural dissenters.

Ferdinand and Isabella had five children; Catherine was the youngest. As royal children their marriages would be determined by the dictates of national policy. For King Ferdinand, the chief danger to Spanish peace and prosperity was King Louis XII of France. The goal of Ferdinand's foreign policy was to secure Spain and contain France, now the most powerful country in Europe, by surrounding it with a series of strong alliances. Isabella, the eldest daughter, went to neighboring Portugal's King Manuel; when she died in childbirth her sister Maria was sent to replace her. Joanna went to the Habsburgs, the family of the Holy Roman emperor — specifically, to Emperor Maximilian's son and heir, Philip of Burgundy. Baby Catherine was promised to England, which was not as important as neighboring Portugal or the powerful empire, but which did have its value in helping to encircle France.

From the Original in the possession of the Honorable Champion Dymoke.

Much of Henry VIII's personality comes through in his letters. His education at Richmond Palace imbued Henry with a respect for the written word, and many of his surviving compositions are eloquent love letters.

Catherine arrived in October 1501, made a splendid impression on the shrewd and guarded king, and in November married Prince Arthur. All England rejoiced, especially young Henry, who distinguished himself in the dancing, as he threw off his coat and frolicked in his shirt and breeches. Not five months later, however, in April 1502, the dynastic and diplomatic plans of England and Spain were spoiled by the untimely death of Arthur. The future of the Tudor line — that fragile grafting of red rose and white that promised peace in England — depended now on a single shoot. The eyes of England — indeed, of all Europe — turned toward young Henry, who succeeded his brother as duke of Cornwall, earl of Chester, and Prince of Wales. Queen Isabella hoped he would also succeed Arthur as Catherine's husband to ensure the Anglo-Spanish alliance. A special dispensation from the pope would be needed to permit Henry to marry his brother's wife, but such dispensations were not uncommon.

In the early part of 1503, in another attempt to provide her husband with more dynastic insurance, Queen Elizabeth died in childbirth. With only one son to stand between the Tudor peace and the civil war that would follow a disputed succession, King Henry thought of taking a new wife to beget more princes. He even thought of marrying Catherine, but Queen Isabella brought the aging king to his senses rather sharply. If the Anglo-Spanish alliance was to have a symbolic marriage, it would have to be that of Catherine and Prince Henry. On June 25, 1503, the two were solemnly betrothed. The wedding was to take place on Henry's 15th birthday, 3 years hence. At Durham House, in genteel poverty and at the mercy of every wind of politics or fortune, Catherine settled down to wait.

Prince Henry's retirement, at Richmond Palace in Surrey, was more strict and isolated than Catherine's. The boy was closely guarded by his nervous father, who was doing his best to keep the last hope of the Tudor line healthy and safe as well as instructing him in the arts and skills that a gentleman and ruler should possess. The prince's chief occupation at Richmond seems to have been tilting, or jousting — the medieval sport of riding in armor, with a lance, against a target or against an opponent with the goal of toppling him from his horse. Henry liked dancing, too, and he seems to have had a real passion and talent for music. Later, at his own court, he would distinguish himself by singing, playing the lute, the flute, the recorder, and various keyboard instruments. He composed songs, too, and even a few masses. He liked reading and argument, and few other English monarchs wrote such fine letters. Prince Henry was deeply influenced by the illustrious circle of learning and culture formed around his paternal grandmother, Margaret Beaufort, countess of Richmond. One of that group was Sir Thomas More, the great humanist scholar. More brought the famous Dutch humanist philosopher Erasmus to see the royal children in 1499, and twenty years later, Erasmus recalled that Prince Henry showed "royalty in his demeanor."

Perhaps the most important influence on Henry's early years was the extraordinary tutor his grandmother chose for him: John Skelton, one of the finest and most original of the great English poets. Skelton wrote that he taught the prince "his letters" and acquainted him "with the muses nine," but the poet's real influence may have been even deeper. The adult Henry possessed a magnificent assurance, energy, warmth, wit, and a colossal appetite for life — the very qualities that leap and dance in Skelton's poems.

Although the formalities in the way of Henry's marriage to Catherine were brushed aside when the dispensation from Pope Julius II arrived in 1504, the death of Queen Isabella shortly thereafter made the wedding much less certain. The lands of Castile passed not to her husband, King Ferdinand, but to their oldest surviving daughter, Joanna, and her husband, Philip. Ferdinand was suddenly a much less important monarch, and his daughter Catherine a much less valuable catch. Ferdinand neglected to send the rest of her dowry, and King Henry

The Dutch humanist philosopher and essayist Erasmus traveled to the English court in 1499. Twenty years later he still recalled the regal bearing of the young Prince Henry.

In 1504 Pope Julius II (shown in a portrait by the great Renaissance Italian painter Raphael) sent a dispensation that allowed Henry to marry Catherine of Aragon, his brother's widow. King Henry VII, however, stalled, trying to find a more advantageous match for his remaining son.

cut off her allowance. To make matters worse, on the day before his 14th birthday, Prince Henry appeared before the Privy Council (the king's advisers; the council carried out much of the functions of government) and secretly repudiated his promise to marry Catherine. Though neither Spain nor Catherine heard of it until much later, the marriage treaty had been unilaterally nullified by the English.

It is unlikely that this was the boy's idea or reflected his wishes. A year later he would refer to Catherine as "my most dear and well-beloved consort, the princess my wife." It was, no doubt, King Henry's desire to explore the possibility of a more advantageous match for his precious son. Indeed he secretly attempted to negotiate a triple wedding with the Habsburgs for himself, Prince Henry, and his youngest daughter, Mary.

Catherine may not have known about the secret renunciation or the Habsburg marriage plot, but she could not help noticing that Henry's 15th birthday came and went without any mention of her promised wedding. Neglected by both Ferdinand and King Henry, Catherine had no money to pay the wages of her little household. She was living with a reduced staff in quarters above the stables at Richmond, and Prince Henry was kept in such complete seclusion that Catherine's ambassador could never manage to talk with him.

Meanwhile, Ferdinand solved his inheritance problems with cunning and boldness. He tricked his son-in-law Philip into naming him regent for Charles, Philip's son. Charles was their common heir; if one died, the other would rule as regent for the boy. Not three months later Philip died; he may have been poisoned. As regent, Ferdinand's hold over Castile was stronger than ever, so Catherine's political value as a bride might have been expected to soar, but King Henry was more interested in arranging his own wedding. He had fallen in love with Catherine's sister Joanna, the bereaved widow. Joanna spurned his appeals, for which he angrily blamed Ferdinand, who, he thought, was trying to keep him from gaining a political foothold in Castile. King Henry made plans to marry himself and his children to Habsburgs. Catherine's prospects were at their lowest ebb when, on April 21, 1509, worn out from his hard and frugal life and already old at 52, Henry VII died at Richmond. The dancing prince was king.

Charles V stood to inherit much of western Europe from his Spanish mother and Austrian father. As Holy Roman emperor, Charles would be a bane to Henry VIII, consistently thwarting the English king's plans on the continent.

3

The Springtime of Sir Loyal Heart

On April 22, 1509, the day after his father died, Prince Henry sprang out of his royal confinement at Richmond to be crowned at the Tower of London as King Henry VIII. It was as if all England had suddenly burst into bloom. The contrast with the old king was immediately apparent in the striking impression the new king made. He was tall, muscular, graceful, and red-cheeked, with soft, delicate, almost girlish features and a natural crown of red-gold hair. The contrast went deeper than appearances. The father, though strong and efficient, had never been popular, his most well-known traits being his frugality and love of money. The son, however, was bright, cheerful, generous, an unusually vital young man, and the merry early years of his reign were a kind of springtime.

King Henry VIII came to the throne amidst great rejoicing, and his first acts increased his popularity. He freed prisoners. He offered to compensate those who had been injured by his father. He had the two

> *[He was] the last of the troubadors . . . a youth wholly absorbed in dance and song, courtly love and knight errantry.*
> —J. J. SCARISBRICK
> British historian, on the young Henry

Handsome, charming Henry VIII came to the throne in 1509 and not two months later married the patient Catherine of Aragon. During the first part of his reign the dashing king spent more time hunting and jousting than attending to the business of government.

hated tax collectors most responsible for building up his father's treasury arrested and executed. He called for dancing and music and assorted merry-making. He instructed the Spanish ambassador to prepare the Princess Catherine for her wedding. Henry did not bring up the secret English nullification of their marriage, nor did he express reservations that Catherine had been his brother's wife. Brushing aside all the long dowry arguments, he made her his queen on June 11, 1509, just short of his 18th birthday (she was 23) in the little Franciscan chapel at Greenwich. Henry reported that this marriage was his father's dying wish. It was more likely his own wish; he seems to have been very much in love.

A wondrous court flourished around this impetuous king and his wise, calm queen. An English friend sent a description to Erasmus: "If you could see how everyone here rejoices in having so great a prince, . . . you would not contain yourself for sheer joy." As if to make up for all his father's strictness, Henry hurled himself into every sort of pleasurable occupation: music and dancing, spear-throwing, mock combat with swords, archery, jousting, even tennis. He loved hunting and hawking and was a superb, tireless rider. Although he found time to be a devout Catholic, too, hearing as many as five masses a day, with additional daily prayers in the queen's chamber, his focus could hardly be said to be on the next world. He loved good food, drinking, rich clothes, gambling at cards or dice, and good company.

The young king loved banquets, pageants with music, and elaborate costume parties called disguisings. In January 1510 Henry and 10 of his friends dressed up like Robin Hood's men and invaded Queen Catherine's chambers, where they forced the queen and her ladies to dance with them before they would take off their masks. At a banquet for foreign dignitaries Henry disguised himself as a Turk. He rode incognito in a knightly tournament at Richmond and had great success. When Catherine gave birth to a son, Prince Henry, on January

He was determined to shine as an intellectual as well as a sportsman.

—JASPER RIDLEY
British historian, on Henry's scholarly interests

1, 1511 (their first baby, a girl, had been born dead the previous year), the jubilant king celebrated with a great tournament at Westminster. He rode in the lists under the banner of "Sir Loyal Heart," and he even wore Catherine's colors, a mark of husbandly devotion extremely rare, if not positively against the rules of chivalry. The merry thanksgiving, however, turned out to be premature — the baby did not live two months.

Despite his appetite for play, the king did not neglect all serious pursuits. He and Catherine particularly enjoyed reading and discussing religious books. He was as keen, curious, and tireless chasing ideas as he was chasing deer. William Roper, the son-in-law and biographer of Sir Thomas More, described how the king would lead More "into his private room, and there some time in matters of astronomy, geometry, divinity, and such other faculties, and some time in his worldly affairs, to sit and confer with him. . . ." Or, Roper says, they would stroll deep in conversation, with Henry's big arm around his learned friend.

Henry did have a darker side. He had a dangerous appetite and could not bear to be denied any desire.

The jousting and celebration organized by Henry VIII to mark the 1511 birth of his son and heir, Henry, is recorded on the Westminster Tournament Roll. The baby died two months later.

Powerful King Louis XII of France caused England, Spain, Venice, and the Holy Roman Empire to unite against him in 1511 when he tried to have Pope Julius deposed. The pope, seeking Henry's aid, promised him the crown of France upon Louis's defeat.

More was quick to recognize Henry's desire for power and the dangers presented by his volatile nature. When Roper marvelled at More's intimacy with Henry, More's response was, "If my head could win him a castle in France, it should not fail to go." But to his subjects, Henry's youthful ebullience and energy seemed fresh and attractive, particularly after the years of Henry VII's self-denial.

In fact the long dream of conquest and glory in France, so long put off by the Wars of the Roses and by Henry VII's sensible concentration on domestic matters, was alive again in the mind and heart of the young king. How could it not be? He loved mock battles and tilting and every sort of sport and play, and his father had never taught him anything deeper about the nature of kingship. Henry played fiercely at all his pastimes; why would he not want to play at what he perceived to be the greatest of all kingly pastimes, heroic war?

The ambitions of England, France, Spain, the Holy Roman Empire, and the papacy clashed in Italy. In 1511 Louis XII of France attempted to have Pope Julius II deposed, and the pope organized the Holy League, with Spain and Venice, against him. Henry's support was important to the Holy League because — thanks to his father's thrift — he was the only monarch in the alliance who had any money. Dreams of glory brought Henry into the Holy League. Ferdinand tempted him with a promise to help him conquer Aquitaine, a vast, rich section of southwest France once owned by the English. Pope Julius even sent a secret bull, or papal decree, naming Henry king of France. The bull would take effect only when Henry had conquered the country.

For his part, Henry promised to help Ferdinand seize the independent kingdom of Navarre on the French-Spanish border. Navarre, of course, was Ferdinand's only goal; he never intended to lift a finger to gain Aquitaine for Henry. The king of Spain ignored the large English army that had arrived in June 1512 to join the promised attack. He invaded Navarre on his own, and when his attack succeeded, his war was over. The English forces, short of supplies and plagued with sickness, finally went home in December, ignoring Henry's orders to stay and fight beside Ferdinand. He did not know Ferdinand was finished fighting. Ferdinand, adding gall to treachery, claimed the English had betrayed him, which gave him an excuse to conclude a quick separate treaty with France.

Undaunted by the humiliating failure of his first military adventure, Henry pressed forward with his war plans. His money lured Emperor Maximilian into the alliance, and a new four-front attack on France was arranged. Henry planned to lead the English troops himself. He was very excited and went to the docks every day to watch his new navy being built. (His 1,000-ton flagship would be popularly called "Great Harry.") To leave a more secure country behind him, he had the Yorkist pretender Edmund de la Pole taken from the Tower, where he had been safely imprisoned for seven years, and beheaded.

Henry eagerly built up the English navy in preparation for his invasion of France. His 1,000-ton flagship, officially titled *Henri Grace à Dieu* was popularly known by the king's own nickname, "Great Harry."

Edmund's brother Richard was already in arms and preparing to fight for the French, who considered the de la Poles the rightful heirs to the English throne.

In the spring of 1513 a large English fleet under Edward Howard set out to harry the French coast and quickly lost two battles. Howard, lord admiral of the fleet, was killed in the second. On June 30 a huge fleet brought Henry and his large army to Calais, the strategic port across the English Channel that had long been held by the English. Henry wore his best armor and rode his huge horse, brought his great bed, and was attended by an incredible number of servants (including 115 men of his chapel). He rode around all night in his armor, cheering the men. He knighted his heroes on the field. He sent noble prisoners back to Catherine. He even got to fire a cannon. He was having the time of his life.

On August 1, the king began a siege of the little town of Thérouanne. His ally Emperor Maximilian came to visit the English camp and made a proposal to Henry: If Henry would pay their wages, he now offered to put himself and the few men he had with him under Henry's command. Henry, thrilled to command an emperor, eagerly agreed. An insignificant but much-bragged-about skirmish, the Battle of the Spurs, took place on August 16, when a body of French cavalrymen accidentally rode up on the English near the town of Guinegate. The Frenchmen fled, leaving behind six standards and a large, unhappy group of noblemen. Henry missed the main action, but when the body of the French force fled, Henry, in wild abandon and assured of victory, galloped after the retreating enemy. Thrilled by the chase, Henry felt like a conqueror. On August 23, Thérouanne surrendered, and Henry generously gave the town to Maximilian, who promptly ordered every building but the little church knocked down. On September 24, after a brief siege, the city of Tournai also surrendered to the English. Henry celebrated his little victories with his usual excess, made plans to come back next year for further heroic adventures, and in October went home for the winter.

He is as eager for war as a lion.

—PAOLO da LODI
Milanese ambassador, on
Henry VIII in 1513

While Henry and most of the English lords were abroad, the greatest battle of his reign had been fought in England. The long-festering border war with Scotland had flared up again. Catherine, designated governor of the realm and captain-general in her husband's absence, along with Thomas Howard, earl of Surrey, commanded the English forces.

The Scottish king, James IV (married to Henry's elder sister Margaret), brought a large army into England, and on September 9, 1513, the English, led by Surrey, engaged him near the village of Flodden. As the battle was joined Catherine was on the road leading a second army north from London, but Surrey did not need her reinforcements. The invaders were crushed, with most of the Scottish lords and the king himself dead on Flodden field.

The victorious English suffered one more casualty than they first realized. Catherine's exertions caused her third pregnancy to miscarry. She bore her misfortune with her customary bravery. She wrote Henry a touching letter, giving him all the praise for England's victories and urging his quick

Henry VIII in full armor sits astride his warhorse. The king's successful sieges of the French towns of Thé-rouanne and Tournai during the summer of 1513 only whetted his appetite for more combat.

return, for without him, she said, "no joy can be accomplished."

When the conqueror of Thérouanne and Tournai arrived home in November 1513 his joys no longer seemed so innocent as they had been. The old pastimes paled beside real combat in France. Henry dreamed of the pope coming to set a new crown on his head in conquered Paris. He and his friends bragged and dreamed and waited for campaigning weather across the channel. Henry raised both his warlords to the rare, high rank of duke: old Surrey, hero of Flodden, became duke of Norfolk; Charles Brandon, Henry's general and second-in-command in France, was made duke of Suffolk. Then the king tried to strengthen the alliance against France with yet another royal marriage, offering his radiant younger sister, Mary, to Charles of Burgundy, the Habsburg heir. Ferdinand and Maximilian both promised once again to join Henry's next invasion. They even went as far as to commit their support in the Treaty of Lille, but 10 days later they both began negotiating secretly with France.

This was the third time Catherine's father had betrayed him, and Henry could hardly believe it. "I do not see any faith in the world," he told the Venetian ambassador to England, "save in me only, and therefore God almighty, who knows this, prospers my affairs." Ferdinand's treachery backfired. Henry turned away from Spain and the empire, which meant turning toward France. King Louis XII, gouty, toothless, and seemingly much older than his 52 years, was delighted finally to make peace with England, and he made his own marriage proposal to prove it. He would marry the delightful 17-year-old Mary himself.

Catherine lost more than political favor in these machinations. Henry, no longer calling himself "Sir Loyal Heart," followed the kingly custom of the day and turned to other women, especially when his wife was pregnant; Catherine accepted this as an unpleasant fact of royal life. After crossing the channel, Henry had raced home ahead of his army to meet Catherine at Richmond, to praise her victory at Flodden and lay the keys of his two conquered towns at her feet. She was soon pregnant again. During this pregnancy, however, Henry had begun an affair with one of the queen's ladies-in-waiting, Elizabeth ("Bessie") Blount, who was soon openly accepted as Henry's mistress.

Catherine found she had another rival, one more ambitious and vastly more dangerous than Blount. One of Henry's men, a priest and a butcher's son named Thomas Wolsey, had displayed such extraordinary ability that he had gained the king's favor. Wolsey had been responsible for preparing the English invasion of France. The subsequent delicate manipulations and negotiations that turned England toward the French after Ferdinand's latest betrayal also had been primarily Wolsey's work. He had such shrewdness, understanding, eloquence, force, and unswerving loyalty that he had replaced Catherine as Henry's first minister, chief adviser, and most trusted confidant. Catherine probably felt Wolsey's usurpation more keenly than Bessie Blount's. In years to come the queen would have even more reason to hate and fear Henry's adviser.

The Great Seal of Henry VIII depicts him as an authoritative king and a mighty warrior. During Henry's sojourn in France, however, it was Catherine who governed England and Thomas Howard, earl of Surrey, who decisively defeated the Scots at Flodden.

4

"Alter Rex" and the Dream of Peace

Wolsey had learned early how to please his king. He found out just what Henry wanted and then used all his considerable powers to achieve Henry's objectives. The loyal, capable Wolsey could handle the Privy Council and outsmart and outmaneuver the foreign ambassadors. Henry could spend less time listening and arguing, and more time with his hawks and hounds. Wolsey rose to be a sort of *alter rex*, or "other king."

His first post was as Henry's almoner (a household chaplain, one of whose duties is to dispense alms), and he made himself useful, fulfilling every task and every mission with such speed and sound judgment that Henry found him increasingly indispensable. The king charged his faithful servant with greater and greater responsibilities, and Wolsey was rewarded with commensurate honors and titles: canon of Windsor, dean of Lincoln, bishop of Tournai, bishop of Lincoln, archbishop of York, and, ultimately, in 1515, lord chancellor of England.

> *This cardinal is king.*
> —SEBASTIAN GIUSTINIANI
> Venetian diplomat, on
> Cardinal Wolsey

Henry VIII consults his Privy Council, a group of ministers and advisers. Throughout his reign Henry tended to entrust enormous responsibilities and administrative control to individuals rather than to his councils. Fortunately, his ability to select talented men proved sound.

Noblemen of Henry's court wait on Thomas Cardinal Wolsey. Wolsey, who rose rapidly to occupy the highest ecclesiastical and secular offices in England, acquired such power that he was called the *alter rex* — the "other king."

With each new title Wolsey augmented his growing fortune. He was made abbot of St. Albans, the wealthiest abbey in the country, and his new palace at Hampton Court was finer and richer than any palace of Henry's, with a staff of some 500 people. In 1515 Pope Leo X, at Henry's urging, made Wolsey a cardinal, the highest ecclesiastical office below the pope.

This first minister and prince of the church in England — Wolsey was the only English cardinal — was a master politician with vast international interests and ambitions. He wanted Henry to be the most important king in Europe, and he desired the glory of engineering a European peace. He also wanted to crown his own labors by becoming pope. He saw a way to increase both Henry's power and his own by moving England away from its treacherous allies and closer to powerful France. When Charles Brandon, the duke of Suffolk, crossed the channel as Henry's representative to the wedding between Mary and King Louis, he also was instructed to discuss joint Anglo-French action against Ferdinand.

Death changed the picture. Eleven weeks after his marriage to the young English princess, Louis passed away. Luckily for Mary, Suffolk, her true love, was at hand to save her from any future polit-

His ambition was not merely to equal but to excel the glorious deeds of his ancestors.

—POLIDORO VERGILIO
papal emissary, on young
King Henry

ical entanglements. When Henry heard that she and the duke had eloped, he was furious, but he was even more deeply troubled by Louis's successor. It was one thing to make an alliance with a French king who was a feeble old ruin, but the new king, Louis's son-in-law Francis I, was a virile, heroic young man of 20 with the same tastes and talents and energies and dreams of glory as Henry. Despite the treaties between their two countries, the two kings were clearly destined to become personal rivals.

Francis showed his mettle promptly. Henry had bragged publicly of his power in the alliance and pompously reassured those worried about the intentions of the new French king. "If I choose, he will cross the Alps," Henry said, "and if I choose, he will not cross." Henry was wrong. Francis, now allied with Venice, crossed the Alps without consulting Henry, sweeping into Italy with a large army. He forced Pope Leo X to sign a treaty at Bologna and resoundingly defeated a Swiss army at Marignano on September 14, 1515. The rich duchy of Milan was now his. In one season Francis had won all the martial glory Henry so desperately desired, and it was more than Henry could bear. A collision between the two was unavoidable.

Alarmed by the new French might, Henry turned back to Ferdinand, signing a defense treaty with Spain that did not provide much opportunity for betrayal. Ferdinand might have found some way to treachery, but he died on January 23, 1516. His grandson Charles — son of Joanna and Philip and grandson of Maximilian — added to his inheritance of Burgundy the kingdoms of Aragon in Spain and Naples in Italy.

Ferdinand's death narrowed Henry's choices. If he wanted to be anti-Valois (the family of the French king) he would have to be pro-Habsburg (the family of the emperor). Maximilian was old and would soon die: Continental Europe would then be dominated by magnificent Francis and awkward young Charles. Bowlegged, stammering, diffident Charles, with his slender body, oversized head, long white face, severely underslung jaw (it caused his mouth

He was of a high mind and loved his own wiil and his own way.
—FRANCIS BACON
English philosopher, on Henry VII

In the image text reads:
IO DNI · 1 5 4 4
MARI
MOST
E HENRI · DOVGHTER TO
THE EIGHT · VERTVOVS PRINC
AGE OF · XXVIII YERES

In May 1516 Catherine gave birth to the only one of her six children who lived. Princess Mary, shown here in a later portrait as queen, was initially doted on by Henry but would suffer bitterly at his hands for much of her life.

to hang open), was not nearly as threatening to Henry as the hearty, athletic Francis was. Because France was England's traditional enemy, Henry leaned toward the Habsburgs. By March Swiss armies in the pay of England stood with the emperor's forces outside the walls of Milan. A major setback for Francis seemed assured, when Maximilian suddenly retreated. Once again Henry's trust in his allies was misplaced.

Fortunately Henry and England were provided with a distraction from foreign affairs. On February 18, 1516, Catherine's fifth pregnancy resulted in the birth of a healthy child. There was some disappointment that the child was a girl, but Henry seemed to dote on her. He bragged to the ambassadors that she never cried. He named her Mary, after his sister.

Henry still wanted to fight in France, with or without the slippery emperor, but Wolsey led him to a peace, at least until England would not have to depend on such unreliable allies. Henry called off the invasion planned for the summer of 1516, but he continued to back France's enemies, including the penitent Maximilian. Wolsey, managing all the monarchs of Europe, engineered a new league to check and contain France. Maximilian took Henry's money and swore his allegiance to Wolsey's league on the four Gospels. On the same day, however, he received a large bribe from the French and soon signed the Treaty of Noyon with King Francis, declaring a Franco-imperial alliance. Henry was "marvellously anguished," according to report. Wolsey wrote the emperor such a furious letter that the English ambassadors decided not to deliver it.

Wolsey's dogged labor and crafty plotting for peace were given a great boost in March 1518, when Pope Leo X proclaimed a five-year truce in Europe. The pope wanted the kings of Christendom to put aside their differences and unite to defeat the Ottoman Turks, led by Selim I, who were threatening at various points around the periphery of Christian Europe. Though Henry thought that the king of France was "one who devises worse things against Christendom than Sultan Selim," Wolsey's own goals were advanced by the papal proclamation. Wolsey had been a cardinal for about three years. He convinced Henry to block the arrival of Cardinal Campeggio, the pope's legate, who came to discuss the truce, until the English church was given its own legate. Unwilling to alienate Henry, the pope agreed, and Wolsey was named a papal legate.

The ambitious cardinal earned his elevation. The pope had called for a five-year truce, but Wolsey in October 1518 negotiated the Treaty of London, by which France and England promised "perpetual" peace. Twenty other countries also signed, guaranteeing the status quo and pledging united action against any aggressor. In a supplementary treaty, England returned (for 600,000 French crowns) Henry's great prize, Tournai, and a match was arranged between Henry's baby daughter, Mary, and Francis's young son and heir, Francis.

Hampton Court, Wolsey's London residence, rivaled Henry's own palaces in luxury. The cardinal greatly enjoyed the trappings of wealth and power, which made him enemies among the resentful nobility.

Henry still hoped for a son of his own, and Catherine kept trying. She had another stillborn child in November 1518. A few months later, the king's prayers were answered in another quarter. His long-time mistress, Bessie Blount, gave birth to a healthy boy. Henry rejoiced openly and named the boy Henry Fitzroy (Henry "king's-son").

In Europe two events — a major dynastic development and an initially obscure religious protest — first complicated and finally doomed Wolsey's great treaty. In October 1517 Martin Luther, a German priest and professor at the University of Wittenberg, had posted on a chapel door 95 theses — points of disagreement with Catholic theology and practice. Those who supported Luther's protests against the dogma and authority of the Roman church would be called Protestants. They intended to reform the church, and their activity helped destroy any idea of a united European Christendom. Wolsey's "perpetual peace" would disappear in the bitter wars of the Protestant Reformation.

The dynastic development had a more immediate effect. In January 1519 death caught up with Maximilian, and the electors — noblemen and church-

English ships carrying Henry and Catherine depart for the June 1520 meeting with Francis I of France at the Field of Cloth of Gold in Flanders. Wolsey planned the gala event to conclude peace between England and France.

men of the German states — got ready to choose the next Holy Roman emperor. Charles, the Habsburg heir and king of Spain, was the logical choice, but Francis I also campaigned vigorously for the office. Henry, with little real chance but with typical optimism, instructed his ministers to lay bribes and exert what pressures they could to make him the next emperor. After all the busy campaigning, the electors chose Charles. The 19-year-old now ruled the largest empire in Europe. The election of Charles V (he ruled Spain as Charles I) marked the beginning of a duel between the houses of Habsburg and Valois that would shatter Wolsey's peace.

Francis found himself surrounded by Habsburg lands — Spain, the Netherlands, Burgundy (eastern France), parts of Italy, and many of the German states — and felt the need for a secure alliance with Henry. The two kings thus planned a meeting to demonstrate their harmony. Cardinal Wolsey was given the unenviable task of arranging the details. It was a very delicate affair, for the two monarchs had to meet as equals, although each undoubtedly would try to outdo the other. Wolsey turned all his administrative skills to preparing one of the most extraordinary and colorful events of Henry's reign — the meeting held between the Flemish villages of Guînes and Ardres at what came to be called the Field of Cloth of Gold.

Henry and Catherine planned to go to France for the whole month of June 1520, making their court at Guînes, which at this time was held by the English. Some 5,000 people — many hundreds in the king's retinue alone — made plans to go with them. Thousands more were already at work in France getting ready for the arrival of the monarch. Craftsmen from England and Flanders joined with French co-workers to build a brick, timber, and canvas palace for Henry beside Guînes Castle that would include a chapel, banquet hall, pantry, and even a cellar. The workmen set up a luxurious pavilion for Henry and erected lists and galleries for the tournaments that would celebrate the meeting. There would be rich costumes and athletic competitions, music, dramatic pageants, and great banquets followed by dancing.

Not everyone regarded the upcoming event as entirely merry. Charles understood that any real harmony between England and France would imperil his various crowns. There did not seem to be much he could do, but warned by his aunt, Catherine, of the proposed meeting, Charles managed to arrange two meetings with Henry himself — one before and one after the great event. Charles respectfully requested permission to pay his respects to his aunt and uncle on his way to pick up his imperial crown, and Henry, flattered, agreed.

Henry and Charles met at Dover Castle on May 27 and the following day rode to join Catherine at Canterbury. With his deferential awkwardness and his self-effacing modesty, the young man made a very good impression on his uncle. He wrote later thanking Henry for "the advice you gave me like a good father when we were at Cantorberi." He seemed like a well-meaning boy who needed Henry's counsel and protection.

The virile young king of France, a worthy opponent for Henry in every way, could hardly be expected to be as deferential to Henry as Charles was. The meeting on the Field of Cloth of Gold was wonderfully dramatic and cordial, with much embracing by the kings. But two things happened — one spectacularly public, the other elusively private — that together sowed the certain destruction of Wolsey's great hopes of English glory. The first occurred when Henry suddenly grabbed Francis by his collar and bellowed, "Come, you shall wrestle with me!" Francis wanted the alliance very much, and he had made every effort to please Henry. The ambassadors had taken great care to keep these eager competitors from riding against each other in the lists, but the surprise of the sudden challenge was too much for Francis: He grabbed Henry, shifted his weight, and skillfully threw the king of England on the grass. The breach of decorum was immediately patched up, but the defeat was an indignity that Henry, so vain of his strength and ability, could never forget. Only a rematch sometime in the future, on the battlefield, could remove the bitter taste in Henry's mouth.

The other "event" was much less specific — in fact, history does not record it precisely — but more significant to Henry and to England in the long run than the entire Cloth of Gold extravaganza. At some point during the merrymaking, Henry is reported to have seen the two daughters of Sir Thomas Boleyn for the first time. The elder girl, Mary, would soon become his mistress. The younger, Anne, would not, and her refusal would sink Wolsey, change the course of English history, and even alter the life of the average Englishman in a very fundamental way.

Wolsey enjoyed his triumph at Guînes. Henry and Francis made each other glorious promises on the Field of Cloth of Gold. Two weeks later, however, there was another familial meeting — at Gravelines in Flanders — between Charles and Henry. Meanwhile, French troops were responsible for a number of threatening border incidents. In August 1521 Wolsey returned to Calais to mediate between Charles and Francis. At Henry's command, he also negotiated a secret military treaty with Charles. The 1518 Treaty of London had committed England to fight any aggressor. Francis was clearly the aggressor in these clashes, and Henry, despite the Field of Cloth of Gold promises, was longing for a war with France. So Wolsey promised Charles everything and then stalled, negotiating feverishly to protect the peace.

Charles, in his efforts to win over the English, assured Henry of imperial support for Wolsey in the next papal elections. As Holy Roman emperor and the nominal secular defender of Christendom, Charles's desires in the election carried great weight. They did not have long to wait: in December 1521 Pope Leo X died, and an enthusiastic Henry looked eagerly to Rome. Wolsey, however, was never seriously considered as a candidate for the papacy by the college of cardinals. A Dutch cardinal, former tutor to Charles, was elected by the college as Adrian VI. The disappointed English were reassured by Charles that the next election would be different.

Henry (right) meets with Charles V, newly elected Holy Roman emperor. Encouraged by Catherine, his aunt, Charles arranged two meetings with Henry in 1520 to thwart a possible Anglo-French alliance.

The emperor, however, probably never intended to support Wolsey's candidacy for pope; he simply needed to secure an English alliance (and money) for as long as possible.

Charles went to see Henry again, in May 1522, and England's long-awaited declaration of war against France soon followed. In June 1523, after more delays and preparations, Henry signed another treaty with Charles, pledging permanent peace and friendship and calling for a joint invasion of France. Henry sealed the pact with the promise of another royal marriage. Seven-year-old Mary, long promised to the dauphin (eldest son of the king) of France, was now pledged to 23-year-old Charles, her cousin, who would wait for her to grow up. If Charles and Mary had a son and Henry had none, the treaty provided that the English crown would be added to Charles's extraordinary inheritance.

In August 1523 a large English army under Suffolk landed at Calais. The English, pillaging freely, besieged the port city of Boulogne, intending to set up a base for the following year's campaign. Boulogne, however, held out, so Wolsey devised another strategy: a march on Paris itself. As most of the French army was tied up fighting imperial troops in northern Italy, Suffolk's troops did well at first, moving to within 50 miles of the French capital, but bad weather, lack of reinforcements, and the usual hardships faced by an army in hostile territory forced a demoralized retreat to Flanders.

The wars of the 1520s caused great changes in Europe. Constant and bitter fighting darkened the magnificent glow of the Renaissance in Italy. With the attention and resources of the monarchs of Christendom focused on mutual destruction, both the Ottoman forces and the Protestant rebels made substantial advances, and the great houses of Habsburg and Valois would ruin themselves in the long struggle.

In September 1523 Adrian VI died. He had been pope for only 20 months. Wolsey's hopes soared, for by now the English, following his plan, had proven their support for Charles by invading France. Henry, too, pouring money into this military venture, felt sure that with Charles's support the papacy was within Wolsey's reach. The king, of course, intended to control Wolsey once he was elected.

This time, however, Charles did not even pretend to put forward Wolsey's name as a candidate, and the cardinals in Rome, afraid of foreign occupation — both French and imperial soldiers were still on Italian soil — elected in November an Italian pope — Giulio de' Medici, a Florentine cardinal from a famous and powerful family, who took the name Clement VII. English hopes for control of the papacy were dashed.

Wolsey, though dismayed by Charles's lack of support for his papal bid, continued with his efforts for peace. He is reported to have urged Charles to renounce his claim to Milan and Henry his old claim to France in order to achieve peace again. Henry, however, remained obsessed by his war, which was not going very well. Suffolk's early victories had turned into a long, draining disaster, and Pope Clement was pressing — with Wolsey maneuvering behind the scenes — for an end to the fighting. Charles was as usual broke and looking for money; Henry had already squandered his large inheritance. Disappointed that Charles had not provided better support to the English war effort or Wolsey's

> *He is so ambitious*
> *So shameless, and so vicious*
> *And so superstitious*
> *And so much oblivious*
> *From whence he came . . .*
> —JOHN SKELTON
> English poet
> from a satire on
> Cardinal Wolsey, 1522

papal aspirations, Henry instructed Wolsey in June 1524 to engage in secret negotiations with France.

An overly optimistic Francis led his army into Italy in October 1524. In late February 1525, at a little town in northern Italy called Pavia, the imperial forces demolished the French army. The chief Yorkist claimant to Henry's crown, Richard de la Pole, was killed fighting with the French. Francis himself, wounded in the cheek and in the hand, was taken prisoner.

The sun came up next morning on a brave new world. Henry could hardly believe it. "You are as welcome," he told the courier who brought him the good news, "as the angel Gabriel was to the Virgin Mary." Wolsey, negotiating with Francis for months, abruptly changed direction and sang a high mass of thanksgiving at St. Paul's Cathedral. Henry reminded Charles that the two of them would one day be united by marriage, and meanwhile, he advised

Henry (right) and Francis meet on the Field of Cloth of Gold at Guînes, 1520. The two kings professed undying friendship and swore oaths of loyalty to each other, but they accomplished nothing of real substance.

him, Francis's very "line and succession ought to be abolished, removed and utterly extinct." Henry in his enthusiasm planned a triumphal entry into Paris. He had a 13-year-old bull from Pope Julius II making him king of France, if he could take it, and his ally had done so.

Mopping up the remaining opposition in France and arranging his coronation would be very expensive, and there was no more money in the once fat Tudor coffers. Henry turned to Wolsey, who invented a levy, known, ironically, as the amicable grant. It would bring to the crown one-sixth of all lay and one-third of all clerical income in England. The English people, docile for 20 years, were sick of war and taxes and suspicious of Henry's adventuring in France. Seeing no evidence of success in France, they did not share Henry's fantasies of conquest, and there was fierce opposition from both commoners and noblemen to the new tax.

Before opposition to the amicable grant broke into an open rebellion, the faithless emperor informed Henry that no imperial troops would aid in the English invasion of France and called off his marriage with nine-year-old Mary. Charles instead agreed to a match with Isabella of Portugal, who would bring him an enormous dowry. Henry would have no French crown and no emperor-grandson.

Galled by the betrayal, Henry at once demanded the repayment of all English loans to Charles — a substantial sum — and abolished the Anglo-imperial treaty. A furious Wolsey threatened an alliance with the Turks, who, making their way up the Danube River, were threatening the eastern regions of Charles's empire.

As he was trying to digest Charles's infamy, Henry received word that his tax collectors were being assaulted, his subjects were paying the amicable grant in cows and chickens, and groups of peasants in rags were begging to be relieved of the levy. Henry was forced to back down, but he regained a measure of admiration when he claimed he had not been consulted on the tax. The English were all too willing to believe that Wolsey had been behind it, although the cardinal said that he had also opposed the grant.

Giulio de'Medici, a member of a wealthy Florentine family, became Pope Clement VII in 1523. Henry had counted on Charles V to support Wolsey's candidacy for the papacy and was bitterly disappointed with the emperor's refusal.

Henry instructed Wolsey to change the direction of his foreign policy once again and make a separate peace with France. The Treaty of the More was signed on August 30, 1525. Five months later Charles made his own peace with France in the Treaty of Madrid. Charles now was the most powerful monarch in Europe. After ceding to Charles the duchy of Burgundy, Francis was freed, but his sons would be held by Charles until a huge ransom was paid. Such Habsburg supremacy would sooner or later lead to renewed fighting, so Wolsey began working to restore the balance of European power by containing the emperor, as Ferdinand had once labored to contain the king of France. In May 1526 the League of Cognac — France, the papal states, Florence, Venice, and the deposed duke of Milan — was formed to check the emperor's power. England, however, refused to join. Wolsey still hoped that England could be the neutral broker of a universal peace.

The league fought with Charles, whose empire was also under fierce attack by the Turks. In August 1526 the Turks under Suleiman the Magnificent defeated the Hungarians at the Battle of Mohács and their path to western Europe was wide open. Charles desperately needed to make an alliance with England. He sent an ambassador to London, but the man was intercepted in France and imprisoned. He arrived too late to prevent another important Anglo-French treaty.

On May 6, 1527, a savage and undisciplined German army under Charles's ally, the duke of Bourbon, sacked Rome. The pope barely managed to scamper down a tunnel from the Vatican to the great fortress Castel Sant'Angelo, where he was now effectively Charles's prisoner.

Wolsey met with Francis and planned a meeting with Charles. He was trying to secure the pope's release, and he was also planning to run the church for him until that could be arranged. Perhaps Wolsey could still achieve a comprehensive European peace, but first he had to attend to another matter. The alter rex always tried to give his king whatever he desired, but what Henry desired now, more than a French crown or an imperial marriage for Mary or even a son from Catherine, only the pope could give him. Henry wanted a divorce.

St. Paul's Cathedral in London was the scene of a joyous mass celebrated by Wolsey upon Henry's receipt of the news that Charles, his ally, had captured Francis at Pavia, Italy, in February 1525. Henry immediately set his sights on the French crown promised him.

5

The King's Great Matter

Henry had long ceased to be Catherine's Sir Loyal Heart. For a king, he had been a relatively faithful husband, given the customs of the period, but there were so many temptations. What ambitious young lady-in-waiting or maid-of-honor, pushed forward perhaps by her relatives to gain a castle or a title, could resist the king's advances? Catherine accepted his philandering during her frequent pregnancies, but so far Henry had always come back.

In June 1525 Henry made Henry Fitzroy earl of Nottingham and duke of Richmond and Somerset. He seemed to be planning to make the boy his heir. The queen protested vigorously at this public humiliation, and Henry responded by reducing her household and dismissing her most faithful attendants. He sent nine-year-old Mary away from her mother to Ludlow Castle, where the young princess of Wales would have her own household and learn her royal duties under the direction of Catherine's good friend, the countess of Salisbury.

It moves me to pity to see how the king's life, the stability and downfall of the whole country hang upon this one question.
—CARDINAL CAMPEGGIO
papal legate on Henry's divorce, 1529

Henry's preoccupation with providing a son to carry on the Tudor line, coupled with a growing passion for Anne Boleyn, led him to seek a divorce from Catherine of Aragon. Frustrated at every turn by Pope Clement, Henry ultimately made the fateful decision to break completely with the Roman church.

Court painter Hans Holbein the Younger made an official portrait of Anne Boleyn as queen. When the seductive, sophisticated Anne first came to court in 1522 she refused to become Henry's mistress, which only increased his infatuation.

The king depended greatly on Catherine, who was his friend and counselor as well as his wife; although he patched up the latest quarrel, his affairs continued. One was with Mary Boleyn, and at some point Mary's little sister caught his eye. Anne Boleyn was a black-haired, long-necked, clever flirt, with an extra nail on her left hand where a sixth finger had started to grow. With her dark almond-shaped eyes and her sophisticated manners acquired over several years at the French court, Anne caused a stir when she came to court early in the winter of 1522.

For whatever reason — girlish modesty, finicky taste, or more mature ambition — Anne refused to become Henry's mistress, and her refusal ultimately rocked England. It is uncertain exactly when Henry began wooing her, but by the time Wolsey began negotiating with the pope Anne was on Henry's mind, although it cannot be said that in the summer of 1527 Henry's sole reason for seeking a divorce was to marry Anne. Anne aspired to be more than the king's mistress, and Henry's desire to have her at any price would have made a divorce necessary sooner or later, but there were other reasons for a divorce. (Although the term divorce is commonly used, what Henry sought was technically an annulment of his marriage — a statement that the union had been invalid from the start. A divorce in the modern sense of the word was strictly prohibited by the church.) Henry still wanted a legitimate male heir. He was relatively young at 35, but Catherine was 41 and worn out by her fruitless pregnancies. A new, younger wife could perhaps give him a son and might also provide more beneficial political connections than the treacherous Spanish-Austrian ties of his first wife. His chief reason, however, was his conscience; he thought his marriage with his brother's wife was against the laws of God. The initial need for the papal dispensation that enabled Henry to marry Catherine was based on the canon, or church, law's prohibition against a man marrying his brother's widow. Henry now believed that the pope had no authority to grant such a dispensation as the prohibition stemmed not from canon law, but from the law of God as revealed in the Old Testament's book of Leviticus. While the pope was the ultimate arbiter of canon law, which was man-made, he had no authority to set aside God's law. Therefore, Henry's marriage to Catherine was invalid, as was the pope's dispensation. That no sons had resulted from Henry and Catherine's union was confirmation to him that he had broken God's law and was being divinely punished.

He must have a divorce, for himself and the fate of his immortal soul; for England, so a proper heir could safeguard the Tudor peace; and most of all for poor Catherine, who had unwittingly been living in sin for 18 years.

Wolsey may not have been enthusiastic about the divorce, which was referred to as "the king's great matter," but he would not despair to be rid of Catherine. She had been his only real rival at court, proudly and shrewdly looking out for the interests of Spain and Emperor Charles. With Catherine out of the way, Wolsey thought that he could marry Henry to a French princess to reconcile the two countries.

Henry had little contact with Catherine after 1524, and once he determined in early 1527 to proceed with plans for the divorce, he hoped to obtain it without Catherine's prior knowledge. In May 1527 Wolsey set up a secret tribunal at Westminster under William Warham, archbishop of Canterbury, to examine the validity of Pope Julius's dispensation originally permitting the marriage. The plan was for Henry to plead guilty to cohabiting with his brother's widow. In his capacity as papal legate, Wolsey would order Henry to separate from Catherine and would invalidate the marriage. Warham, who had been a trusted counselor to Henry VII, was fearful and stubborn. Catherine, after all, could appeal any verdict to the current pope, who although her nephew's prisoner, was still head of the church. Charles was not likely to favor a divorce, which would allow his aunt to be cast aside and raise the specter of an Anglo-French marriage alliance sometime in the future. The secret tribunal disbanded without reaching a decision after three sessions, and it was determined to try to convince the English bishops and then the pope of the validity of Henry's arguments. Wolsey was dispatched to the continent to press the King's case.

On June 22, 1527, after stalling as long as he could, Henry gave her the news. Their marriage was invalid, sinful; they would have to separate. She wept, but then she responded. If he had doubts, she said, they must certainly be resolved, but she had none. She might live apart from him, she would go wherever he sent her, but she would always be his true wife, and she would always remain queen of England.

She was firm and brave, but also desperate. She knew she had to get word to Charles before Wolsey and Pope Clement could betray her. Henry and Wolsey were determined to prevent any message from getting through. One of her attendants, Francisco Felipez, who had entered her service 27 years earlier as a page, offered to carry her message to Charles. Travelling by sea, the brave Spaniard managed to elude the agents Henry sent to stop him and reached Charles in his castle at Valladolid, Spain. Charles reacted firmly and swiftly. He sent Henry a plain, vigorous protest. He promised Catherine his full support, and he pressed Catherine's case to the captive pope.

In France, Wolsey pursued his own strategies. He believed diplomacy could be used to obtain the pope's consent to an annulment and at the same time achieve other ends. If Wolsey could achieve his dream of peace in Europe through negotiating a treaty between France, England, and the Holy Roman Empire, then presumably Clement would be freed to take up the matter of Henry's divorce. If neither could be achieved, then Wolsey hoped to gather the support of the cardinals to allow him to exercise the papal authority, and he would rule on the matter.

Wolsey had little luck with either Charles or Francis. Neither was much interested in his mediations for peace, and Clement thought the idea of Wolsey temporarily running the church was a greater danger than his own continuing imprisonment. In addition, the cardinal was losing control of matters in

A nervous Wolsey looks over his shoulder as Henry woos Anne. Relations between Wolsey and Anne's family were tense from the start; each side resented the other's hold over Henry.

England. Henry, having broken publicly with Catherine, turned openly to Anne. Impatient with Wolsey's strategy, Henry sent his own emissaries to Rome, asking for a special dispensation to have more than one wife and for a special dispensation to allow marriage with Anne. Wolsey's interference with Henry's envoys and the persistent talk that Wolsey favored a marriage between Henry and French royalty increased the king's irritation with his chancellor.

The king believed that Wolsey was unenthusiastic in his "great matter," and he began to distrust the alter rex. Yet Wolsey continued to serve his lord, even proposing a more convincing argument for obtaining the divorce. Henry had been arguing that Catherine's marriage to his elder brother had been consummated; Catherine vehemently denied it. Wolsey now suggested that even if the marriage had never been consummated, Pope Julius had sent the wrong dispensation. If Catherine left Arthur's bed a virgin, then she and Henry had needed a dispensation "for public honesty," that is, to undo a marriage publicly promised or contracted but never consummated. The pope's dispensation for "affinity" — for a consummated relationship between a couple too closely related — would be invalid and so, too, would the marriage.

Henry continued to ignore Wolsey's slow strategies, and the cardinal knew he was in trouble. Anne and her relatives, especially her uncle Thomas Howard, duke of Norfolk (son of Surrey, the victor at Flodden), were scheming to bring about his downfall. Wolsey sent Henry an uncharacteristically pitiful note — "there was never a lover more desirous of the sight of his lady, than I am of your most noble and royal person" — and hurried home from France. When he got there, he was not allowed to see Henry alone. Anne, smirking and sneering, was present at all their interviews. He might still dream of a French alliance, but now he took orders from Anne.

In December 1527 Clement managed to escape from Rome to the little town of Orvieto and thus gain some measure of independence from Charles, but he was not ready to make a decision on Henry's marriage. The drama of the king of England's divorce took place against the background of enormous changes within Europe, as the Protestant Reformation, sparked by Martin Luther, shook the temporal and spiritual authority of the church. At the mercy of the armies of competing European powers, threatened by the ground swell of a rising religious revolution, the pope vacillated. To Clement, a clever, timid pragmatist, it seemed safest to make no choice for the time being. He used all his considerable skills and talents to obstruct and delay. He gave one of Henry's frequent ambassadors a dispensation for Henry to marry Anne, but there was a catch: the dispensation could take effect only if the marriage with Catherine was ruled unlawful. Henry fell back to square one.

In January 1528, with a weakened Wolsey still dictating English foreign policy, England declared war on the emperor. Wolsey hoped to reduce Charles's power in Europe, win Francis some relief from the harsh terms of the Treaty of Madrid, gain (in the long run) a universal peace, and secure Henry's divorce. Clement began his own negotiations with Charles. The news frightened Henry; an alliance between Catherine's nephew and the pope would certainly not help him obtain his divorce.

In March 1528 Stephen Gardiner, a royal secretary, and Edward Fox, Henry's almoner, pressed Clement to set up a decretal commission, a tribunal that would have the power to decide the king's great matter once and for all. The two tough ambassadors even hinted that the beleaguered pope might be risking Henry's allegiance and that Henry was considering breaking with the church. There was great irony in this. In 1521 Henry had written a book against Lutheranism, *The Defense of the Seven Sacraments*, in which he resoundingly affirmed, among other things, the indissolubility of marriage and the primacy of the pope. For this service, Leo X had named him Defender of the Faith. Now if Clement would not give him a divorce, Henry's advisers intimated, the defender would leave the fold.

Clement knew how to look like he was giving in without giving away anything at all. Instead of the

A well-protected gate at the Tower of London leads into a section called the Bloody Tower. As Henry's rage over his inability to obtain a divorce mounted, he showed no scruples about imprisoning his opponents.

requested decretal commission, he set up a general commission. Wolsey and Lorenzo Cardinal Campeggio would hear Henry's case in England, and there would be no appeal from their verdict. Gardiner and Fox were overjoyed. This time Clement's catch was that papal confirmation of the verdict was not guaranteed.

Wolsey and the king were grieved not to have a full decretal commission, and they sent Gardiner back to Rome to try and obtain it. In October 1528 Campeggio brought with him to London the precious decretal commission, so the two legates could decide the question themselves, or so Henry thought. In fact, Cardinal Campeggio lacked the proper documents and had orders to stall. Some change in the international situation might make the crisis disappear. Catherine might die, for example. Henry might get tired of Anne, or Anne might give in. Henry himself might die. Clement preferred to wait as long as he could and see what might happen. Wolsey confronted the gout-stricken Campeggio in his sickbed and threatened a breach with Rome if the commission delayed further.

So Campeggio bestirred himself. First, before the trial could begin, an effort had to be made to reconcile the couple. Then Campeggio suggested that the problem could be solved without a messy trial if Catherine would agree to enter a convent. Henry thought this a great idea, and Wolsey begged for it on bended knee, but Catherine said she had no religious vocation and would stay in the holy state of matrimony to which God had called her.

Campeggio's report to the pope was pessimistic. He said that "an angel descending from heaven" could not change Henry's mind, and that Catherine was willing to be torn to pieces, rise up, and be torn to pieces again for what she believed. How could she feel otherwise? To give in was to betray her whole life: her parents' hopes and wishes; her long, bitter wait after Arthur's death; her happy years of being Henry's wife and England's beloved queen; her young daughter's rightful succession; and even, perhaps, the hope of peace in England after Henry's death. Catherine also felt she would endanger her immortal soul — it was a sin to lie. Campeggio was running out of ideas for stalling. He advised Clement to recall the case to Rome.

Catherine then suddenly produced a copy from Spain of a second dispensation from Julius II for her marriage with Arthur. Though it made the same point as the dispensation the pope had originally sent to England, its language was slightly broader. If the document was not a forgery, the Campeggio-Wolsey commission was, at least temporarily, ended. Their mandate referred only — and very specifically—to the dispensation in England.

Henry was wild. He had to get his hands on the "Spanish" brief, either to prove it a forgery or to do away with it. So he forced Catherine to send a letter to Charles telling him that unless the actual document was produced in the English court it would be judged a forgery and asking him to please send it "for her sake and her child's." Furthermore, Henry made Catherine swear on pain of treason to send no other letter than this one.

She had sworn not to send a letter, but she could still send a messenger. Francisco Felipez dared to ride off again, but this time he came back two weeks

After several delays the divorce trial of Henry and Catherine began in May 1529. In June Catherine knelt dramatically before Henry to plead her case directly to him, but Henry was unmoved.

63

later with a broken arm. It turned out to be the official messenger — Thomas Abell — who came to Catherine's rescue. Abell, the man carefully selected by Wolsey to carry the letter to Charles, on his own authority drew up a methodical summary of reasons why the emperor should ignore the request for the original document. He pointed out that a notarized copy of the Spanish dispensation would satisfy the English court, and he made a list of steps Charles could take to help prevent the divorce. After finishing his conscientious embassy, Abell returned to England. He brought the notarized copy of the dispensation with him. Then he sat down and wrote a powerful treatise opposing Henry's case. For his courage and principles, Abell would spend six years in the Tower and then lose his head to Henry's executioner.

Though Catherine seemed weak, she had powerful allies. Charles's armies dominated Europe, and their victories won a secret promise from the pope: the divorce case would not be decided in England. The queen also commanded the devotion of allies dearer to Henry than the emperor: the English people. They cheered her whenever they saw her, and they began to turn against Henry. Most of all, they hated Wolsey, unjustly blaming him for everything. In November 1528 Henry addressed a group of hostile Londoners and told them of his fears and scruples. Nothing would please him better, he said, than for the court to find his marriage with Catherine valid. "If I were to marry again," he said, "*if* the marriage might be good, I would choose her above all other women."

In December 1528, Henry had Catherine moved out of her chambers at the palace at Greenwich, and Anne moved into quarters near Henry's. In February 1529 a report reached England that Pope Clement was dead. Henry and Wolsey immediately focused their attention on getting Wolsey elected to succeed him, but the report had been premature. Clement had miraculously recovered from a severe illness, and in March Catherine wrote asking him to try her case in Rome. Campeggio, sick and low on funds, begged the pope to call the case to Rome. Henry, who by now had waited two years for Anne, pressed Campeggio to act. Finally, the pope could delay no longer and ordered the trial to begin. The legatine court convened on May 31, 1529, at Blackfriars. Neither Henry nor Catherine attended the opening discussions. It was not until June 18, the day of her defense, that Catherine appeared to plead her case. The dignified queen protested the judges and appealed to Rome. Henry sent a proxy. The real drama came three days later. Henry and Catherine were both present, but before the session could begin, Catherine walked over to her husband, knelt before him, and begged him not to cast her and her daughter aside. She also asked him, on his conscience, to tell the court whether or not she had come to him a virgin. He refused to say anything at all. She arose and departed with dignity. "This is no indifferent court for me," she said. "I will not tarry." She never came again. When she had gone, Henry gave his familiar speech about his troubled conscience. Then Wolsey knelt and asked the king to tell the court if he, Wolsey, was "the chief inventor or first mover of this matter." Henry replied he was not.

In Catherine's absence, her lawyers did little to defend her. The one exception was John Fisher, the bold bishop of Rochester, who declared his unwavering support for the queen. Catherine's best defense lay in her nephew's armies, and on June 21, the very day Catherine knelt before Henry at Blackfriars, they won a decisive victory over the French at Landriano, Italy. France had now lost Italy, and Henry's worst fears were soon realized. Pope Clement signed the Treaty of Barcelona with the emperor. Meanwhile, the English court was bogged down with arguments about such technicalities as the authenticity of the Spanish dispensation.

One month later Clement revoked the legatine court at Blackfriars and called the case to Rome. Wolsey heard this bad news before Campeggio did, and he had a slim, desperate hope that the court would hand down its decision before the Italian cardinal learned of the pope's decision. He had not reckoned on Campeggio's own skill at stalling. Cam-

> *The whole Church is subject not only to Christ but . . . to Christ's only vicar, the Pope of Rome.*
> —HENRY VIII
> from *Defense of the Seven Sacraments*, 1521

Wolsey turns over his palace at Hampton Court to Henry, 1530. The cardinal's quick fall from power was due to the failure of his foreign policy, enemies at court, and Henry's anger over the still undecided matter of his divorce.

peggio surprised his fellow legate by suddenly adjourning the court. Since it was an official Roman court, Campeggio pointed out, it would take the customary Roman summer holiday. Wolsey's hopes were crushed.

Worse was yet to come. Another of Charles's aunts, Archduchess Margaret of Austria, regent of the Netherlands, had been meeting with King Francis's mother, Louise of Savoy, at Cambrai. They were attempting to negotiate a peace between Charles and Francis. Wolsey had assured Henry that it would come to nothing, but the hapless cardinal was wrong again. On August 5, 1529, "the Ladies' Peace" — the Treaty of Cambrai — ended the war between France and the empire. In March 1530, Clement crowned Charles at Bologna. The Habsburg empire was truly a Holy Roman Empire again. Universal peace was achieved not through Wolsey's machinations, but by isolating and abandoning England. Wolsey's wide-ranging, multifaceted foreign policy was as great a failure as his complicated, energetic divorce strategy. His ruin was complete.

Henry refused to see him. The courtiers, who always despised him for his low birth, high arrogance, and pro-French policies, were delighted to keep him away. He retired in despair to his London residence, York Place. The Court of King's Bench indicted him on charges of violating *praemunire* statutes by trying to establish papal legal supremacy in English courts. In October his two old enemies, Norfolk and Suffolk, demanded the surrender of the Great Seal of his office.

Henry confiscated Wolsey's beautiful palace at Hampton Court and then stole York Place, which Wolsey held as archbishop of York, the only position remaining to him, and which should have descended to his successor in that office. In the spring of 1530 Wolsey withdrew north to the city of York. Wolsey wept and prayed, repented, put on hair shirts, sent Henry letters and presents, plotted and begged. One of the cardinal's men, Thomas Cromwell, tried to buy his master favor (and favor for himself, too) by doling out bribes from Wolsey's great fortune.

When Henry heard in late October that the pope had forbidden marriage with Anne before the case was decided, his former chancellor bore the brunt of his wrath. On November 4, 1530, at his dinner in York, Wolsey was arrested for treason, for intriguing "both in and out of the kingdom" and for "presumptuous sinister practices made to the Court of Rome." The cardinal unwisely had corresponded with Francis, Charles, the pope — anyone he could think of in an attempt to alleviate his plight.

On November 29, in Leicester Abbey, on his long journey back to London for trial, Wolsey cheated the executioner and died in bed. In London, when the cruel, triumphant Boleyn family heard the news, they had a new farce, entitled *Of the Cardinal's Going to Hell*, performed for the delight of the court.

> *If I had served my God as diligently as I have done my King, he would not have given me over in my gray hairs.*
> —CARDINAL WOLSEY
> after his arrest in 1530

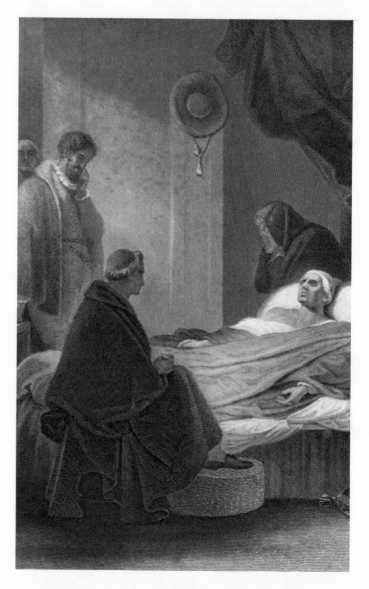

On his way to London to be tried for treason (and probably executed), Wolsey died at Leicester Abbey in November 1530. The delighted Boleyn family held a farce to celebrate their hated enemy's demise.

Catherine and Anne were living in different wings of the palace at Greenwich, and Henry was at his wits' end. One memorable night, after losing another argument with Catherine, he went to Anne seeking consolation. Equally disconsolate, Anne screamed and wept. She was tired of waiting — and so was Henry. "If the pope does not decide in my favor," Henry told Catherine, "I shall declare the pope a heretic and marry whom I please."

Such a "heretic" pope could excommunicate the king, direct all Christians to shun him, even declare the reward of a heavenly blessing — an indulgence — to anyone who murdered him. Furthermore, Henry's subjects were Catholic, and they loved their Catholic queen. Defiance of the pope was a bold step, and it was uncertain that the English people would support him. To support Henry against the pope might endanger their own souls. Having destroyed the powerful Wolsey, would the once devout king challenge the authority of the pope?

THE
Historie of the
REFORMATION
of the
CHURCH of ENGLAND

RELIGION

SUPERSTITION

THE
HOLY
BIBLE

THE POPE

PIPES
DECREES

6

The Reward of Virtue

The fall of Wolsey left several sizable gaps in Henry's administration. Wolsey's energy and ability had served Henry in every way. His Eltham Ordinance of January 1526 had introduced crucial economies and reforms in the running of the court, streamlining the royal household. Superfluous attendants were released; those who had ably served the king were duly promoted. Wolsey had known how to form and carry out a complicated plan. He had been lord chancellor, the architect of English foreign policy and of the complex ecclesiastical maneuvers aimed at securing the divorce. Henry would sorely miss the very capable civil servant. He needed to find an equally talented man, another giant, to replace him.

Henry quickly picked such a man to succeed Wolsey as chancellor, his old friend Sir Thomas More. More tried to decline the office. He had kept a discreet silence about "the king's great matter"; he had tried to avoid an open conflict over Henry's pragmatic theology, which inexorably was evolving away from Rome. Henry said he understood, and he promised that More would always be free to follow

I wish to command only my own subjects; but on the other hand I do not choose that anyone shall have it in his power to command me.
—HENRY VIII

On this cover for a history of the Reformation in England Archbishop Thomas Cranmer (right) points to Henry as Supreme Head of the church as both tread underfoot the symbols of papal authority. In the background the building of the true religion continues as the foundation of superstition is torn down.

After Wolsey's fall Henry appointed Sir Thomas More chancellor. The king promised that More would be free to follow his conscience. When More did so, it cost him his life.

his conscience, so More accepted the Great Seal. It was not a promise that Henry would be able to keep. To manage England's foreign policy and secure his divorce — the two things had become nearly synonymous — Henry needed a man who would not be affected, as the earnest, scholarly More was, by his conscience. He found his man, fittingly, in the ruins of Wolsey's establishment. Thomas Cromwell had served Wolsey well, particularly in squeezing various religious houses to provide funds for the cardinal's own projects.

There was much anticlerical feeling in England, much hostility to the power, wealth, pomp, and high-handedness of a church badly in need of reforming. Wolsey's fall from power only seemed to fuel the fires of the secularists. Henry did not create this feeling, but he was glad to make use of it. In November 1529 Henry called for a Parliament, a gathering of representatives from all over England, to help him solve his problems with the church. Made up of both lords and commoners, this Reformation Parliament would be the instrument of great

Unwilling to trust one man again, Henry divided Wolsey's responsibilities, but Thomas Cromwell, a "new man" who owed his advancement solely to his service to the king regarding his divorce, would quickly come to be as indispensible to Henry as Wolsey had been.

changes in England. The brilliant, pragmatic, ruthless, indefatigable Cromwell would be its master. He would soon come to be Henry's most valued adviser.

Another man, though hardly a giant, also tumbled forward to take up a share of Wolsey's work. Thomas Cranmer, a mousy young priest working as a tutor, had devised a plan for polling the universities of Europe to drum up some prestigious support for Henry's divorce case. Henry liked the plan, and by early 1530 English ambassadors were running a huge public relations campaign on the continent. As principal royal secretary Cromwell would be Henry's chief secular minister; Cranmer would serve as the English leader of a much devalued church.

As he was changing his ministers, the king of England was also developing grave reservations about certain aspects of the faith he once so publicly defended. He was much taken with a book entitled *The Obedience of a Christian Man*; the author, William Tyndale, was a leading Protestant reformer and argued that a king had absolute authority over all his subjects.

He is so blindly in love that he cannot see his way clearly.
—DIEGO HURTADO
DE MENDOZA
Spanish ambassador, on
Henry VIII

Thomas Cranmer became archbishop of Canterbury in 1533, but his first loyalty was to Henry, not the pope. Cranmer aided Henry in separating the English church from Rome.

Soon Henry was asserting that no Englishman, especially the king, could be brought to trial in Rome. Henry insisted that his case must be settled in England. He instructed his ambassadors in Rome not to consent to papal jurisdiction. They were afraid even to mention Henry's claims to the pope, but Parliament was already demanding specific reforms of the church in England, and some of Henry's nobles went so far as to assert that the king himself was "absolute emperor and pope" in his kingdom.

Wolsey had invented complicated strategies to pry a divorce from the pope. Cromwell developed a bold, simple plan to win it from the English people. Cromwell wanted both houses of Parliament (the House of Lords and the House of Commons) and Convocation — the council of English ecclesiastics — to join in certifying Henry as head of the church in England. Henry could then grant his own divorce. In January 1531 Henry terrorized the churchmen meeting at Canterbury with trumped-up treason charges, threatening to try them for violations of the praemunire statutes. If he chose, he could seize all their property and have them put to death. To mollify him, the churchmen voted to donate 40,000 crowns to his treasury. He rejected their offer. They raised the ransom to 100,000 crowns. This he accepted, but he also insisted that they acknowledge him as "Supreme Head of the Church and Clergy in England." They could not, of course, agree to this. John Fisher, for one, would not let them and thundered fearlessly against what he perceived as Henry's tyranny. It was weary old Archbishop Warham, the leader of Convocation, who invented the compromise that saved them, for the moment. They were willing to call him Supreme Head "so far as the law of Christ allows."

In Henry's Parliament there was surprising support for the frightened clerics. The legislators could see the danger to themselves in a wholesale use of spurious treason charges. John Fisher, who had denounced the divorce case, was also a member of the House of Lords and the outspoken leader of Henry's opposition in that body. In 1532 Henry's minions pressured Parliament to support the king's divorce, but the members resisted. Henry sent them home for six months.

Unable to get what he wanted by bullying pope, emperor, Convocation, or Parliament, Henry tried again with Catherine. Early on the morning of July 11, 1531, Henry and Anne left Windsor to go hunting. They did not return that night. Instead Henry sent word to Catherine to leave the court; her suite was to be reduced. She was not to attempt to write to the king, and she would no longer be allowed to see her daughter. Catherine answered with a humility that veiled a wonderful threat. She would go anywhere he wished, but she would prefer to be sent to the Tower, so that the people could see what had happened to her and would give her their prayers. Henry did not even say good-bye when he rode away from his wife of 22 years; he would never see her again.

Henry knew very well the enormous good will the people held for their queen; he could not put her in the Tower. Catherine was sent away to a succession of variously isolated and uncomfortable houses. Anne's star kept rising with Henry, but the people hated her, and they were beginning to hate Henry, too. Behind the scenes, Cromwell was organizing his spies and his secret police, wheedling, pressuring, bribing, placing his men in important posts, plotting to influence Parliament to support the king. He could not yet get the House of Commons to break decisively with Rome, but he could get them to take a big step in that direction by attacking the privileged English clergy. Cromwell himself wrote the draft of the "Supplication against the Ordinaries" (ordinaries were the judges in the ecclesiastical courts) — a long collection of complaints against the church that was revised by the House of Commons and sent to the king in March 1532. The bishops in Convocation stood firmly against the Supplication. All abuses ought to be corrected, they responded, but the church would not surrender its independence. Henry discovered another threat to his authority: papal oaths. Priests at their consecrations swore oaths to the pope. Were they then

> *His aim . . . was to make the King supreme over every phase of English life.*
> —WILL DURANT
> American historian, on
> Thomas Cromwell

true subjects of the king? Henry asked Parliament "to invent some order, that we be not thus deluded of our spiritual subjects."

On May 15, 1532, frightened by Henry's threats of possible parliamentary action against them, the bishops of Convocation, with John Fisher sick at Rochester and some other leaders also absent, surrendered. At this "Rump" Convocation, so called because the absence of its leading members made it an ineffectual remnant of a true council, the Submission of the Clergy stated that all future church laws or regulations would have to be approved by the king; all past rulings would have to be reviewed for his consent. The day after the Rump Convocation surrendered the independence of the English church, Sir Thomas More resigned his office. His conscience would no longer let him serve Henry, but he would still not publicly oppose him. He had two more years of troubled silence left. The title of chancellor would go to other men, but the power of the office stayed with Cromwell.

Another man of principle moved belatedly to break his silence. Archbishop Warham had always been afraid. His early advice to Catherine had been succinct: "The wrath of the king is death," he had warned. Even in his eighties he still feared death enough to have voted with the Rump Convocation. Unaccountably, Warham changed his mind. He announced that he would move in the House of Lords for the repeal of all the recent laws against the church. Henry accused him of treason. In his defense, Warham reminded the Parliament of another priest who had stood up to his king: St. Thomas à Becket, who had been martyred at Canterbury, Warham's own see, by the barons of another King Henry, over the issue of the liberty of the church. "And if in my case, my lords, you think to draw your swords and hew me in small pieces, . . . I think it more better for me to suffer the same," he declared, than to give way to the present Henry. It is unlikely that Henry VIII's barons would have behaved much better than Henry II's, but Warham eluded them. He died in his bed in August 1532.

The post of archbishop of Canterbury is the most important spiritual post in England, and it was es-

> *If all the patterns and pictures of a merciless prince were lost in the world, they might all be painted to life, out of the story of this King.*
> —SIR WALTER RALEIGH
> English courtier and
> author, on Henry VIII

sential for Cromwell and the king to fill it with their own man. They selected the innocuous, easygoing scholar who had suggested polling the universities, Thomas Cranmer. In October 1532 Henry sent ambassadors to Rome to secure the pope's consent to this appointment.

But the long negotiations, the crafty strategies and cunning delays, the years of frustrated patience were all at an end. Henry could not even wait to see if the pope would let Cranmer, so eager to help him, become archbishop of Canterbury. The long, long wait was over. Anne was pregnant.

The death of Warham and the promise of a speedy resolution seems to have melted Anne's resistance.

Henry married a pregnant Anne Boleyn in a small, secret ceremony in January 1533. Henry did not obtain his divorce until that May, when the compliant Cranmer annulled his marriage to Catherine. A series of laws severing the English church's ties with Rome followed shortly thereafter.

After six years of smoldering virtue, she let her royal sweetheart have his way. Perhaps she acted to keep Henry from looking around for a more suitable bride, now that he was almost free. A week after the old archbishop's passing Henry suddenly had raised Anne to be marchioness of Pembroke, with lands and title to descend to her "heir male." The usual stipulation in such cases, that the "heir male" be legitimate, was omitted. Henry remained unconcerned about the universal antipathy to his elevation of Anne to the nobility, for he hoped that Anne carried the next king of England in her womb. To ensure the baby's legitimacy, on January 25, 1533, in a secret ceremony, Henry, as yet undivorced, was bigamously married to Anne.

The pope was not warned about the secret wedding, and he still hoped to mollify Henry. If he could not give him his divorce, he could at least give him his own archbishop. Clement could not know what a disaster the appointment of Cranmer would be for the church in England. Clement's approval came, and on March 30, Thomas Cranmer swore his public oath to the pope as the new archbishop of Canterbury. He had taken the precaution, four days earlier, of swearing a secret oath of primary loyalty to Henry. In April the new archbishop wrote the king begging to be allowed to settle the divorce case. The king gave him permission.

Another embassy was sent to Catherine. Norfolk and Suffolk begged her to give in; if she refused, she would be taken prisoner. Her allowance would be greatly reduced, and no one would be allowed to address her as queen. She would have to be called the princess dowager, her title as Henry's widowed sister-in-law. Catherine said she did not care about her allowance, but any who served her must continue to call her queen. Before he left, Norfolk, who pitied her, told her that she might as well give up: Henry had married Anne.

On April 5 Convocation ruled the king's marriage to Catherine unlawful. John Fisher, the only bishop to protest, was arrested the next morning. Cranmer painstakingly tried the case at the Priory of St. Peter in Dunstable, and on May 23 the archbishop ruled

that Catherine's marriage to Arthur had been consummated; her marriage to Henry was, therefore, null and void. Back in London, on May 28, after sincere reflection, Cranmer further ruled that Henry's secret marriage to Anne was good and valid. On June 1, Anne paraded with great pomp to Westminster, where Cranmer crowned her queen. It is reported that the people along the way called out, "God save Queen Catherine." Ten days after Anne was crowned, Pope Clement solemnly but secretly condemned Henry's separation from Catherine and his new marriage to Anne. On July 11, Clement excommunicated Cranmer and the bishops who worked with him on Henry's divorce. He also prepared a secret bull against the king. If Henry did not take Catherine back by September, Clement would excommunicate him also.

Henry's bad luck continued. On September 7, 1533, Anne gave birth to a little girl. The king, not even attempting to hide his dismay that it was not a boy, did not attend the child's christening. He named the child Elizabeth, after his mother.

Spurred by Cromwell, Parliament passed a series of laws in 1533–34 that effactually ended all connection between the English church and Rome. The Act in Restraint of Appeals declared that all English cases, including, of course, the king's divorce, had to be tried in England, without further appeal to any higher earthly authority. Five more major laws

The coronation procession of Anne Boleyn at Westminster Abbey in June 1533. The new queen was almost universally despised by the English people, who believed that she had bewitched Henry.

The heads of the recently executed Thomas More and Bishop John Fisher were displayed on pikes on London Bridge (shown here in a 1751 sketch) in the summer of 1535. The two had refused to swear allegiance to Henry as Supreme Head of the English church.

affecting the church were passed in the first parliamentary session of 1534. The Act of Dispensations required that all dispensations and licenses be supplied in England, not sent from Rome. The Act of Succession established any children the king had by Anne as first in line to inherit the crown, and included an oath to be administered throughout England by which the English people would acknowledge as valid both the marriage to Anne and the new statutory rights of her offspring. The Act in Absolute Restraint of Annates ended all payments to Rome for benefices — church offices that provided clerics with money or goods to make a living — and also gave the king sole power to appoint English bishops. The Act for the Submission of the Clergy formalized the surrender of authority and independence agreed to by the Rump Convocation. The Heresy Act permitted Englishmen to deny the doctrine of papal primacy.

In April 1534 Thomas More and John Fisher refused to take the succession oath and were sent to prison in the Tower. Catherine also refused to take the oath, but Henry dared not send her to the Tower. Nineteen-year-old Mary furiously refused the oath, too, although she was repeatedly bullied, threatened, and even subjected to physical violence to get her to swear. Henry did not dare put his own daughter in the Tower, either. Eustace Chapuys, the imperial ambassador, was terrified that mother and daughter would be poisoned by Queen Anne. In fact, among the commoners it was thought Anne was a witch and a poisoner.

In November 1534 Parliament outdid itself with an act more explicit and revolutionary than all the others. The Act of Supremacy was the culmination of Cromwell's labor. The Act of Supremacy simply recognized Henry as the Supreme Head on earth of the English church. A new Treason Act soon followed: "malicious denial" of the king's supreme headship was punishable by death. The break was irreparable — the Roman Catholic church had lost England.

"The wrath of the king is death": many must have remembered old Warham's warning. Among the first to earn the king's wrath by denying his supremacy were five Carthusian monks, brave gentlemen cruelly executed — hanged and disemboweled — in May 1535. John Fisher was next. On the day of his execution, June 22, 1535, he put on his finest clothes, telling his perplexed servant that this was his wedding day. As if to taunt Henry, Fisher's gaunt, reproachful head, stuck on a pike on London Bridge, stayed amazingly lifelike, convincing the people of the bishop's holiness. A month later Sir Thomas More followed Fisher. Despite More's long and cunning silence the king was well aware of his former chancellor's scruples. At the end, More was convicted only by the lies of a man named Richard Rich, who swore that More had spoken treason while in the Tower. "I die the king's good servant," More told the crowd at the scaffold, "but God's first."

If Cromwell's policy of terror and judicially sanctioned murder helped make Henry safe in his fearful power, another policy made him rich. In the winter of 1534–35, Cromwell's men had painstakingly inventoried the great wealth of church property and revenue in England, and in 1536, slowly but surely, they began to steal it for the king.

By this time Cromwell had streamlined much of the government in London. In fact, many of his administrative and financial reforms would prove far-reaching, surviving both him and Henry. Cromwell increased the independence of the Privy Council, making it a body capable of running the court on

> *We thought that the clergy of our realm had been our subjects wholly, but now we perceive that they be but half our subjects, yea, and scarce our subjects.*
> —HENRY VIII
> on the conflict between allegiance to the crown and to Rome, 1532

its own as well as dealing with foreign affairs. He expanded the role of the king's secretary to include financial responsibility for the royal household. In 1536, as money began to come in from the dissolution of the monasteries, Cromwell began the reorganization of the treasury, dividing it into six main offices in order to increase its efficiency.

Cromwell's reforms made for a more self-sufficient government, but the king still remained the authority behind it all. Yet Henry had his mind on other matters. Anne was pregnant again in the autumn of 1535, and he hoped to finally have a son. Anne had greater reason to pray for a son, for she had become aware that the king was not in love with her any more. Her failure to produce an heir — Anne had suffered two miscarriages after Elizabeth's birth — seemed a mocking insult to Henry, and people were saying that the marriage was cursed. Anne's own family, aware that Henry was growing tired of her, had brought her cousin Madge Shelton to court in the hope that she would amuse the monarch and keep the family in power. Henry took the bait. When Anne complained, Henry sharply told her that she would just have to learn to accept it, "as one of her betters had done."

Henry forgot all about Madge Shelton when he saw Jane Seymour. Jane, the daughter of one of his knights, was a very pale woman in her mid-twenties, not thought to be particularly pretty or accomplished by any but the lovestruck king. Her affectionate rejection of the king's advances had its usual effect: It endeared her to him.

Unfortunately, Catherine did not live to see the downfall of her usurper. She died in lonely poverty on January 8, 1536. On her deathbed she wrote a letter to Henry professing her love for him, forgiving him, urging him to think of his soul, begging him to be a good father to Mary, and asking him humbly to take care of her few faithful maids, as she had nothing to leave them. "Lastly, I make this vow," she wrote, "that mine eyes desire you above all things." She had not seen him for nearly five years. He had not permitted her to see her daughter in that time, either, although she often begged him for that privilege.

Jane Seymour was a quiet, gentle woman from a family of the lesser nobility. As Henry grew estranged from Anne, he began to court Jane, who demurely resisted his advances.

When Henry heard Catherine was dead he put on a suit of yellow satin with a white feather in his cap. Anne, also dressed in yellow and pregnant again, celebrated with the king. Their merriment, however, was short-lived. Henry nearly followed Catherine before the month was out. On January 21, while riding in the lists at Greenwich, Henry took a great fall. He was knocked off his horse, and the horse, with all its heavy armor, fell on top of him. As the king lay unconscious for two hours court held its breath. There were three royal children, only one male, the illegitimate Henry Fitzroy, and two female, one the disinherited 19-year-old daughter of the rightful queen, the other the 2-year-old heir apparent. There was also another royal child on the way. All these children would have some supporters, despite the Succession Oath, and the old dynastic wars could come again if Henry died.

Queen Anne begs the king to hear her case. Only three years after his marriage, Henry repudiated Anne and her daughter, Elizabeth. Cromwell charged Anne with treason (by reason of adultery) and in May 1536 the queen, protesting her innocence, was beheaded.

Henry recovered from this accident, but Anne did not. The unhappy queen had no real friend except Henry, and she knew even he had grown tired of her. A week after Henry's fall, on the very day Catherine was buried, Anne lost her baby, a boy. Her great fear for Henry was the cause, she said. The angry, disappointed king was not much impressed with her explanation.

Shortly thereafter Henry decided his second marriage was also invalid. He had been seduced by witchcraft, he said. Cromwell's spies laid traps to collect evidence of treason by Anne. Meanwhile Henry sent Jane Seymour a love letter and a purse. Though she made a great show of kissing the letter, she sent it back unopened with the purse and a touching message about her family's honor and her own unsullied virtue. Henry vowed to protect that virtue. Anne was increasingly in his way.

Cromwell's minions gathered their evidence. Under threat of torture, a young musician named Mark Smeaton confessed that he had made love to Anne. Then at a May Day tournament she was seen to drop her handkerchief to the king's old friend, Sir Henry Norris. Norris was arrested, and so was his friend George Boleyn (Lord Rochford) — Anne's brother. Two other friends of Henry's were also indicted. Anne was sent to the Tower, tried on the treasonous charges of adultery and incest, found guilty, and sentenced to death. Henry celebrated the sentencing with a merry pageant on the river. On May 18, 1536, Anne watched from her window as her supposed lovers, including her brother, were beheaded on Tower Green. The following day, still protesting her innocence, Anne Boleyn, Henry's great love, went to the block. She put her hair up to improve the executioner's aim, and she joked that her little neck would not cause him much of a problem.

Archbishop Cranmer had already officially determined that the marriage between Henry and Anne was invalid because of Henry's earlier affair with Anne's sister. On the day Anne died Cranmer provided Henry with a special dispensation to marry Jane. Henry spent the day quietly at home. On the next day, he was engaged to Jane Seymour.

7

The Lonely Bridegroom

With both his queens dead, Henry was essentially free. In fact because both marriages had been annulled, he was technically a first-time bridegroom when he exchanged his vows with Jane Seymour in a quiet ceremony at York Place on May 30, 1536.

Anne's death had freed Henry to marry again, but Catherine's death had freed him, too, in the wider world of international politics. The death of Pope Clement in October 1534 raised intriguing possibilities. The new pope, Paul III, was thought to be more principled and resolute, but the threatened excommunication of heretical Henry had still not been announced, and there was some hope that the differences between pope and king could be resolved. Neither of the popes nor the emperor had been willing to act against Henry without a direct appeal from Catherine, and by the time she determined to ask Pope Paul for a "remedy" — in a letter of October 1535 — the time for action was past.

God has not only made us King by inheritance, but has given us wisdom, policy, and other graces in most plentiful sort, necessary for a prince to direct his affairs by honor and glory.
—HENRY VIII
1536

A later portrait of Henry VIII shows an enormous, dissolute man prematurely aged from his excesses. Once Henry discovered he was accountable to no one, he ravaged the English church by ordering the dissolution of the monasteries, using the money he acquired on pointless wars in France.

Reginald Pole was the member of the Yorkist family with the strongest claim to the English throne. As Henry was besieged at home with a widespread popular rebellion, the Pilgrimage of Grace, over his dissolution of the monasteries, Cardinal Pole settled in Flanders to stir up discontent against the king.

Three months later Catherine was dead, and the emperor, who could hardly have ignored an excommunication and a papal call to arms to defend the honor of his aunt, was no longer eager to quarrel with Henry.

The church lost more in England than the hearts and minds of the people. The enormous wealth of the English monasteries, so carefully recorded by Cromwell's men, was, according to Henry, wealth that properly belonged to the crown. The excesses of the independent, greedy, powerful churchmen called out for reform, but it was the riches that attracted Cromwell and his master. The job of reforming the monasteries — that is, robbing, dissolving, pillaging, and destroying — begun in 1536 was making Henry wealthy again.

The effort was not unopposed. The specter of civil war loomed again as various rebellions broke out — confused and separate actions to defend the old church and oppose both the new heresies and the low-born ministers, including Cromwell and Cranmer, who were thought to be misleading the king. The uprisings began in the eastern and central counties of Lincolnshire and Yorkshire, spread throughout the north and northwest, and were known collectively as the Pilgrimage of Grace.

It was a perilous time for Henry, because it was hard to imagine where he might turn for support. The Pilgrimage could spread all over England or encourage attack from Scotland. Pope Paul cunningly raised the old dynastic threat by naming the surviving Yorkist claimant to the English crown, Reginald Pole, a cardinal.

The leaders of the uprisings believed that Henry was being misled by his advisers and that he would quickly redress their honest grievances. They did not know Henry. He was furious, threatening "the utter destruction" of "beastly" Lincolnshire and of the rebels and their families. When he saw the breadth and depth of the revolt, however, he tried another tactic. At a conference held in Doncaster priory in early December the rebels presented a comprehensive petition including requests for a general pardon and redress of their grievances in Parliament. Henry's representative, the duke of Norfolk, promised them satisfaction, and the rebels joyfully dispersed.

Nonetheless, a new wave of trouble in Yorkshire gave the king all the excuse he needed for brutal revenge. He had been quietly preparing the royal troops for this, and in the early part of 1537 his soldiers descended on rebel strongholds in the north and west, destroying property, hanging and burning the so-called traitors. Despite the promised pardons, the leaders were tried in London and then sent back to their homes in chains, to be executed in May.

Henry had survived the most serious domestic troubles of his reign, but they gave him a taste of what might lie ahead for England when he died. A compliant Parliament had gone along with his plan to disinherit Mary and pass the crown to the children of his marriage to Anne, but the Pilgrimage of Grace revealed how much support Catherine's daughter still had in England, and the only child of his marriage with Anne had been rendered illegitimate when that marriage was nullified. A further threat to peace in his realm lurked somewhere on the continent in the person of Cardinal Pole, the Yorkist pretender. Henry tried to resolve this problem by wringing another Succession Act out of Parliament. This one gave him the surprising power to appoint his own successor. Perhaps he planned to pass his crown to Henry Fitzroy, his son by Bessie Blount. Unfortunately, the king's strange bad luck still held. Not a month after the act was signed, the young duke died of tuberculosis.

Henry's grief was soon followed by rejoicing and then by greater grief. On October 12, 1537, Queen Jane presented Henry with a proper son and heir, Edward. Henry was not there at the birth — he had fled to escape an epidemic — but he hurried back to Hampton Court to begin the celebrations. Jane, however, was unable to recover from the childbirth, and 12 days later her death left the king a lonely widower.

> *The Pilgrimage must stand as a large-scale, spontaneous, authentic indictment of all that Henry most obviously stood for; and it passed judgment on him as surely and comprehensively as Magna Carta condemned King John.*
> —J. J. SCARISBRICK
> British historian, on the Pilgrimage of Grace

In October 1537 Henry received the son he so desperately wanted. Prince Edward was cause for great celebration, but to Henry's immense sorrow Queen Jane Seymour died nearly two weeks later.

Henry seems to have been genuinely in love with Jane, but he was not one for dwelling on the past and grieving excessively. Word went out on the day Jane died, and a week after she was buried Henry's ambassadors in Europe were actively seeking her successor. The great search went on for two increasingly frantic years before ending in disaster.

Henry's youthful, romping appetite for a new wife was comic because he was no longer the man he used to be. A long way from the innocence, grace, and springtime promise of Sir Loyal Heart, he was fat and coarse, notoriously selfish, and a willful, cruel, and dangerous monarch. But he still thought himself a great prize, and he conducted his wedding sweepstakes like a huge, vulgar beauty contest. He thought of taking a French bride, the king's daughter, perhaps. Henry sent one of his famous court painters, Hans Holbein the Younger, to do a portrait of the widowed 16-year-old duchess of Milan. Every new possibility titillated Henry, who behaved like an overgrown boy in a candy shop, and he sent painters off to do pictures of each bridal candidate.

The situation became much less merry in the summer of 1538, when Charles and Francis, who had been fighting in Italy for 2 years, signed a 10-year truce at Nice and then met at Aigues-Mortes to consider some joint action against the spreading Protestant heresies. Neither Habsburg nor Valois now needed a marriage with England, and both considered Henry a threat to Catholic unity in Europe. Pope Paul III, taking advantage of Henry's isolation, in December released the three-year-old brief excommunicating Henry. The English people were now, according to the pope, free to disobey their king.

In January 1539 Charles and Francis pledged not to make separate agreements with England, and Henry prepared for war. One of the first moves of the frightened Tudor was to vanquish all potential domestic rivals. He attacked three distinguished noble families — the Courtenays, the Nevilles, and the Poles — executing men, imprisoning and executing women, and even having some children secretly murdered. Even the Poles' distinguished matriarch, the elderly Margaret Pole, countess of Salisbury, was beheaded on Tower Green in 1541 after a long imprisonment.

Searching desperately for allies, Henry made overtures to the Protestant leaders of Germany, who had banded together in the League of Schmalkalde. These Lutherans were cool to the imperiled monarch, who after all was not exactly a true Protestant. They knew Henry was not interested in serving any "true" religion, only in presenting himself as the earthly embodiment of it. Although a few reformers, including John Calvin, had sided with the king in his "great matter," Martin Luther had called the divorce "a crime in God's sight." "Squire Henry means to be God and do as he pleases," Luther observed with disdain.

To secure an alliance, however, Henry now pretended to be more interested in Lutheranism, even as Parliament, expertly managed by Cromwell, was attempting to arrest the spread of radical Protestantism in England. In May 1539 Parliament passed the Act of Six Articles, a codification of the basic principles of the new Anglican church, which put a stop to further Lutheran reforms. Under the Six Articles, the Anglican church kept much of the Catholic doctrine; the difference was that the English church was headed by the king, not the pope. In the central conflict between Catholicism and Lutheranism over transubstantiation, Henry adhered to the Catholic position that the communion bread and wine is miraculously changed into the actual body and blood of Christ during the mass. Any dissenters from this belief were now subject to punishment; Henry was not ready to tolerate radical Protestantism in his realm. Yet at the same time the conservative Six Articles became law, the ruthless and methodical spoiling of the rich English monasteries continued. Twenty-six wagon loads of treasure were carried away from the famous shrine of St. Thomas à Becket at Canterbury, and the bones of the saint were cast away.

As the German princes turned from Henry to make their own peace with Charles, the star of another bridal candidate rose. The young duke of

Henry views a favorable portrait of the German princess Anne of Cleves. After the sad death of Jane, Cromwell maneuvered the king into a political alliance with the strategically located German state.

Cleves (a German duchy), who stood, like Henry, somewhere between Catholicism and Lutheranism, was quarreling with Charles and was not allied with the Lutheran states. The duke had two unmarried sisters, and Henry sent Holbein off to paint their portraits. He heard good reports of the elder sister, Anne.

There were also less favorable reports warning that Anne of Cleves had little education, few accomplishments besides sewing, no language but German, and that she was provincial and quite dull. Cromwell may have kept these opinions from reaching Henry, for he wanted the alliance. A marriage treaty was concluded, and Anne arrived at Rochester Abbey on New Year's Eve, 1540. Great festivities were prepared at Greenwich, but Henry could not wait. He galloped down to Rochester the following day to see his new bride.

"I see nothing in this woman as men report of her," he lamented afterward, "and I marvel that wise men would make such reports as they have done." He did not even give her the furs he had brought as presents. "If I had known as much before as I know now," he told Cromwell — with whom he was particularly displeased for having talked him into this union — "she should never have come into this realm." For a week Henry tried to find a way out of his predicament, but the treaty was signed, the international situation was grave, and England sorely needed the alliance with strategically situated Cleves. The wedding day, January 6, 1540, was a bleak one for old Sir Loyal Heart. "If it were not to satisfy the world and my realm, I would not do that I must do this day for none earthly thing," he declared.

The royal couple did not live happily ever after. Henry told Cromwell that marriage did not make him like Anne any better, so he consoled himself by falling in love with someone else. His new interest was one of Anne's maids-of-honor — the small, round, merry, and very beautiful Catherine Howard, another niece of Norfolk. She had been brought to court, in fact, by that determined aristocrat for the express purpose of consoling the king. Catherine was 19, 3 years younger than Henry's daughter Mary.

It was a dangerous moment for poor Anne. In addition to the personal dislike the king had for her, the international circumstances that had brought her to England were changing, and not to her advantage. The old conflict between Charles and Francis was starting up again, and if the rival houses of Habsburg and Valois came to blows Henry would be courted. He would need no alliance with Cleves.

It was a dangerous moment, too, for Thomas Cromwell. He had served the king faithfully and brilliantly, as Wolsey had, succeeding where Wolsey failed. Cromwell had forged the alliance with Parliament that brought Henry his divorce. His cunning, ruthless parliamentary strategies, bureaucratic thoroughness in assaulting the monasteries, and comprehensive administrative reforms had been most effective. Now, however, Cromwell had failed as Wolsey had failed, in that most important of English domestic policies, managing the occupants of the royal bed.

This now famous picture of Anne of Cleves, painted by Holbein the Younger, persuaded Henry to marry her before he had even met her. Cromwell may have stifled reports less flattering about Anne so as not to jeopardize the alliance.

Henry recoils upon his first look at his bride-to-be, Anne of Cleves. The king disliked the German princess from the start but was compelled to honor his word to marry her. The two were wed in January 1540.

In April 1540 Henry rewarded Cromwell for all his good services by raising him to be earl of Essex and great chamberlain of England, but he also told his chief minister to get him out of his marriage. Cromwell delayed. He did not know quite what to do. Perhaps he did not realize how great his peril was. Not two months later, the captain of the guard interrupted a meeting of the Privy Council to arrest the astonished chancellor. Norfolk stripped him of his decorations, and he was taken to the Tower. He was charged with various sorts of treason, and the evidence against him included more testimony from Sir Richard Rich, the perjurer who had helped convict Sir Thomas More.

It is still not clear why Henry let Cromwell fall. He seems to have acted rashly, carried away by Norfolk and the lords who hated Cromwell for his low birth and position of virtually unlimited power. Henry's desire for Catherine Howard was increasingly urgent, and he must have resented Cromwell for saddling him with Anne.

With Henry as head of the English church, divorce was no longer a problem. Cranmer presided over a trial that took two days, and the marriage proved invalid on the grounds that Anne had been promised previously to the son of the duke of Lorraine. It was also determined that Henry had never really consented to this marriage; the proof was his inability to consummate it. The six-month-old marriage was declared null and void on July 7, 1540. Anne meekly accepted the verdict, for which Henry gratefully gave her two houses and a handsome allowance. The alliance with Cleves was broken. For the rest of her life, Anne lived quietly in England. She and Henry became friends, in fact, and sometimes dined together.

On July 28, in a quiet ceremony at Oatlands, a manor house in Surrey, the royal bachelor married the vivacious Catherine Howard. She had only been at court eight months. The triumph of the nobles was complete, for on the day of the wedding Thomas Cromwell was beheaded at the Tower. The bewildered minister summarized his career simply before he died: "As for the commonwealth, I have done my best and no one can accuse me of having done wrong wilfully." Among her wedding presents, Queen Catherine received the greater part of Cromwell's lands. Six months later, in a black mood, Henry would miss him and recall him as "the most faithful servant" he had ever had.

Two days after Cromwell's execution, the king had three leading Protestant reformers burned as heretics at Smithfield. Their real crime was to have been associated with Cromwell. The same day, three unreformed Catholics, including Thomas Abell, who had courageously served Catherine of Aragon, were also executed. Henry seemed to be indicating that his church would steer a middle course between Protestant and pope.

If Henry never got to live happily ever after, it certainly was not for lack of trying, but his new queen was not a good match for an old king. Catherine Howard would have loved Henry's springtime; she liked dancing and flirting and, it seems, making love. She was no innocent when Henry wooed her, and she did not long remain faithful to him. He was 30 years her senior, grossly fat, with an ulcerous leg that pained him greatly. His dancing days were done. At 49 he was a cranky, swollen, sagging invalid, given to fits of explosive rage when laid up with fever and the draining of his leg. Catherine quickly grew bored and melancholy. Partly to entertain her and partly to fulfill an old plan made at the time of the Pilgrimage of Grace rebellion, the king proposed to make a "progress" — that is, to take the court on a great state visit — to the north, a part of his kingdom he had never seen. Henry wanted to judge for himself the mood of the region, for the northern counties were staunchly Catholic and notoriously independent. The additional lure of a possible meeting at York with his nephew, King James V of Scotland, helped Henry decide to go. The Great Progress, which began in June 1541 and lasted 4 months, was a spectacular show: 5,000 horsemen and 1,000 foot soldiers accompanied the king and court. Catherine found her own entertainment,

[He is] the hardest friend to bear in the world—at one time unstable, at another time obstinate and proud . . . the strangest man in the world.
—FRANCIS I
king of France (1515–47),
on Henry VIII

Shortly after Henry married Anne of Cleves, pretty, vivacious Catherine Howard caught his eye. Although Anne calmly agreed to a divorce, Henry held Cromwell responsible for the whole disastrous affair, and the minister's downfall was ensured.

however, in the person of a young courtier named Thomas Culpeper. With the help of one of the queen's attendants, Jane Boleyn, Lady Rochford (the widow of Anne Boleyn's executed brother), Culpeper paid secret visits to young Catherine at every stage of the long progress.

Although the meeting with James did not take place and the king remained concerned about the unsettled relations with the Scots, Henry was mostly pleased with the Great Progress and felt that he had won the loyalty of his subjects in the north.

When Henry returned to London he ordered special prayers of thanksgiving, both for his safe return and for his good life with his new queen. On the following day Archbishop Cranmer handed Henry a paper documenting Catherine's extramarital adventures. Henry violently rejected the charges at first, but more and more horrors came out, including the dalliance with Culpeper. Henry called for a sword to murder her himself. He promised she had never had "such delight in her incontinency as she should have torture in her death."

Culpeper and Catherine's former lover, Francis Dereham, were arrested, tried, found guilty of treason, and executed. Catherine and Lady Rochford were beheaded on February 13, 1542. An Act of Attainder was framed to protect poor, pitiful Henry, who "regretted his ill-luck in meeting with such ill-conditioned wives," by making it treason for any unchaste woman to marry him in the future or for anyone to conceal such a woman's past.

Norfolk, no doubt stupefied that a second niece could leap so quickly from the king's bed to the executioner's block, disowned the guilty queen, absented himself from court, and begged Henry's pity and forgiveness. He kept his head, at least for the time being, even if he gave up his dignity and some of his power to do so.

The prospect of meeting with King James V of Scotland helped convince Henry to travel to the north of his kingdom in June 1541. Henry was pleased with the Great Progress, as the trip was called, but upon his return he was presented with evidence of Catherine's adulterous behavior.

8

The Long Winter

This time the lonely bridegroom made no immediate effort to find a new mate. Other royal pleasures were safer, and he turned to a long neglected amusement: war. In July 1542 another installment began in the interminable Habsburg-Valois conflict, and Henry was courted by both emperor and king. He was in his element, negotiating to match his daughter Mary with Francis's son and at the same time planning with Charles a joint attack on France. The old dream of conquering France had recaptured the king's imagination, and he made plans to lead another campaign. This time, however, he meant to protect his rear before he sailed to Calais. Scotland, in uneasy fealty, might try again to take advantage of his absence, and he had no warrior-queen this time to leave behind.

Henry had hoped to settle the Scottish situation while on his northern progress. After King James failed to meet him, Henry tired of trying to lure him south or woo him with diplomacy. An English army under Norfolk made a short but violent raid in October, and in November a large body of Scottish troops fled from the English forces after a brief battle

Henry and his sixth and final wife, Catherine Parr. Obese and ailing, Henry spent his last years concocting fruitless, labyrinthine diplomatic moves abroad and implementing destructive policies at home. His unpredictable behavior toward those around him at times bordered on the sadistic.

In July 1543 Mary Stuart was the infant queen of Scotland. Henry proposed to betroth her to his son and heir, Edward, in the hope that such a union would finally subdue the rebellious Scots.

at Solway Moss. Many prisoners were taken in this Scottish disgrace, and King James died a few weeks later, leaving his one-week-old daughter, Mary Stuart, as heir.

Henry hit on a scheme to subdue Scotland once and for all by joining the crowns through a marriage of the children. He would be little Mary's protector, and she would be married to Edward. Though the Scottish nobles were fiercely opposed to English involvement in their government, a treaty was signed in July 1543. Henry had hoped to be in France by this time, but the Scots had delayed him.

The emperor, his potential ally against France, also hindered him. Henry and Charles wanted to mount a joint attack on Francis, but they had trouble coming up with an acceptable treaty. The Holy Roman emperor, supposedly the champion of the Catholic church, could hardly forge an alliance with a king who insisted on calling himself Supreme Head of the church. Nevertheless, acceptable language was found, and an Anglo-imperial treaty was signed in February 1543.

The triumph over Scotland and the preparations for war on the continent had made Henry feel young again and in need of a wife. Catherine Parr was a 31-year-old widow, virtuous, pleasant, intelligent, and deeply devout. Perhaps Henry realized that he had more need now of a nurse-companion than of a pretty young childbearer. He married his sixth wife — his third Catherine — on July 12, 1543. It was the most sensible match he had made since his first one, 34 years earlier. Catherine Parr was an exceedingly good, generous, tolerant woman. As a result of her persistent efforts, for example, the three royal children came together in their father's house for the first time. Anne of Cleves came, too, and occasionally had dinner with Henry and Catherine. The new queen, a Protestant, was something of a scholar, and she delighted in popular works of piety and devotion. Henry's court soon shone again with the joyful pursuit of learning, as it had in the early days of Catherine of Aragon's graceful patronage.

Henry had little time to celebrate his marital felicity. He was too busy planning his attack on

France. He was also preoccupied with the rapidly deteriorating situation in Scotland. The regent for Mary Stuart, James Hamilton (Lord Arran), who had signed the treaty with England, was beset by factions hostile to the English and soon went over to them. Henry decided to wage war on Scotland in September. The Scottish parliament annulled the treaty, and Scotland renewed its old alliance with France. Henry sent an army under Jane Seymour's brother, Edward Seymour, Lord Hertford. Hertford had orders to attack and destroy Edinburgh, the capital, knock Scotland out of the war with France, and set Henry up as "Protector of the Realm" and "Chief Governor" of Mary Stuart. Hertford advised against such a bloody strike, but Henry insisted. The resulting raid united and rallied the Scots, exactly as Hertford predicted.

Preparations went on for the French invasion. Henry came to Calais for the last time on July 14, 1544. He and Charles had planned a joint attack on Paris, but Henry had given Norfolk orders to lay siege to the little town of Montreuil instead. When the king arrived he began another siege, with Suffolk, at Boulogne. The English surrounded the city on July 15, blew up the castle on September 11, and entered the conquered citadel on September 18. Henry had a terrific time. He still naively believed that it was not too late for him to be king of France.

The emperor could not, of course, extract similar sustenance from Henry's fantasies. All he knew was that the campaigning season was over, and the agreed-upon strategy — the capture of Paris — had not been carried out. Francis had dangled offers of peace before Henry, but the king was too intent on the siege at Boulogne to consider them. He spurned Francis's offers and dutifully reported them to Charles. The emperor, however, was more realistic and signed the Treaty of Crépy with Francis on the day Henry entered Boulogne.

Henry went home full of wrath but still planning to come back and campaign the following year. When he heard that Norfolk and Suffolk had pulled most of their men out of Boulogne, Henry was livid. He ordered them to go back, but they were lucky to

Henry married Catherine Parr in 1543, less than a year and a half after Catherine Howard was executed. Like his first wife, she was a practical, good-natured, and caring companion.

Henry possessed the undefinable quality of majesty, the ensorcelling aura of kingly command and fatherly authority that overawed his subjects and gave his enemies pause.
—CAROLLY ERICKSON
American historian

101

A Protestant, Catherine Parr spent much time discussing theology with Henry. The queen's religious arguments seemed to steer Henry toward adopting a more radical Protestantism, alarming many of his clergymen.

get their men home from Calais. Whether he wanted to or not, Henry had to negotiate with France. Moreover, the treacherous Charles, who had steered him into this mess, now offered to be the mediator to get him out of it.

Henry needed the help. The English had made countless raids across the Scottish border, and at Melrose, in the early part of 1545, desecrated the tombs of the ancestors of Archibald Douglas, earl of Angus, who attacked the English at Ancrum Moor and beat them. Two French armies were heading for Scotland for a joint invasion of England. King Francis, at peace now with Charles, was also free to attack the south of England. Henry was at odds with Charles, had no allies among the princes of Germany, and had made an enemy of the duke of Cleves. A papal council that could rally Christendom against him now seemed imminent. To top off his troubles, he was broke. No wonder he regretted murdering Cromwell; he desperately needed a shrewd minister.

An armada of 200 French ships did actually attack, landing on the Isle of Wight on July 21, 1545, but they did little damage and soon sailed home again. Perhaps Francis only wanted to frighten Henry. The French king may have understood that a real invasion cost much more than it could ever be worth—a lesson Henry never learned.

Henry hated having to make peace with France. He was especially reluctant to give back his prize of Boulogne. He tried desperately to rally Charles to fight again. He offered all his children as bait for Habsburg marriages. Charles, however, was preparing to smash the Protestant princes in Germany; he was not interested in Henry's proposals.

The German princes, threatened by Charles, now turned to Henry and Francis for help. Henry, taking advantage of the moment, sent a large army under Hertford back to France but then inexplicably changed his mind and made peace with Francis on June 7, 1546. Henry's diplomatic maneuverings became more and more complicated and obscure. He promised aid to the German princes, tried to get Charles to join him in an attack on Francis, and planned a major invasion of Scotland.

At home Henry received an ambassador from Pope Paul, who was attempting to achieve a reconciliation between Henry and the Roman church. Yet the king seemed to be moving toward a more Protestant stance, preparing another purge of the church — he needed the money — and claiming he was worried about the spiritual state of the nation. His resurgent Protestantism may have resulted from the influence of his queen and her circle, but powerful, conservative currents ran against her reforms. The bishop of Winchester, Stephen Gardiner, long one of Henry's leading ministers, was brutally hunting down Protestant heretics. One of his victims was a gentlewoman named Anne Askew, a reformer in London who had much sympathetic support among the queen's ladies. She refused to affirm that the Communion sacrament was the actual "flesh, blood, and bone" of Christ, and for this heretical opinion she was burned at Smithfield, one of the first great Protestant martyrs of England.

Henry with his eldest daughter, Mary, and his court jester, Will Somers. Through the efforts of Catherine Parr, the king was reconciled with Mary and Elizabeth.

Gardiner and his conservative allies hoped the fall of Anne Askew would help them ruin the heretical queen, whose favorites were their enemies. Henry's increasingly erratic behavior encouraged Gardiner. Present one day when the king suddenly cut off Catherine's usual flow of doctrinal chatter and complained of being "taught" by his wife, Gardiner soon after accused the queen of heresy and persuaded Henry to sign a secret bill of articles drawn up against her. Ignorant of her peril, Catherine continued her usual wifely attempts to inspire Henry to further reforms of the church. When she discovered the plot against her she hurried, weeping, to the king to beg his mercy and forgiveness. Genial and condescending, Henry made up with her. When Gardiner's men came to arrest her the following day, they were astonished to find Henry defending his wife. He roughly berated the very men with whom he had been plotting.

There seems to be little reason for this melodrama, but it was not an isolated case. Henry had grown exceedingly devious and somewhat sadistic. He liked power, and one of the things he liked best was power's ability to inspire fear. Henry played with the people close to him as a cat plays with captured

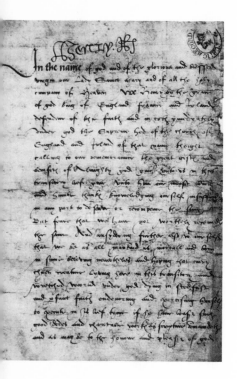

Henry VIII died in January 1547. He settled the succession in his will, fully expecting that his son, Edward, would continue his rule. Ironically, though, it would be his neglected daughter Elizabeth, last in line to the throne, who would bring renown to the Tudor dynasty.

mice. Sometimes they got away; sometimes he bit their heads off.

As Henry's health failed the Howards saw their influence wane as the power of the Seymours increased. The forces striving for dominance made the court a dangerous place. In December 1546 Norfolk's enemies brought both him and his son Henry, long a favorite of the king, to the Tower. At his trial it was charged that the son had boasted of his royal Plantagenet blood, a treasonable offense to the Tudor King, who viewed such boasts as potential claims to the throne. Henry Howard was beheaded on January 19, 1547.

Norfolk tried to save himself with a groveling "confession." A Bill of Attainder seized the Duke's lands and goods (most went to Edward Seymour). And the man who had toppled Wolsey and Cromwell, who had survived the execution of two royal nieces and now his own noble son, was waiting in the Tower on the morning of January 28, 1547, to be led to his own beheading when it was discovered that Henry, attended only by the faithful Cranmer, had died earlier that very morning.

Henry had reigned for 37 years. He was buried at Windsor beside Jane Seymour, the only wife he had not divorced or beheaded and the mother of his son and heir. His heir, Edward VI, lived only six more years, just long enough — under the severe protectorship of his uncle, Lord Hertford — to establish Henry's unique brand of Protestantism, Anglicanism, in England. The boy died of the tuberculosis that felled all the Tudor men except Henry. He was succeeded by his half sister Mary, Catherine of Aragon's much-abused daughter, who tried to restore her mother's Catholic faith with a vengeance that earned her the nickname Bloody Mary. Many English Protestants, including Thomas Cranmer, were executed during Mary's reign. Cardinal Pole, the Yorkist pretender, returned in triumph from his long years of plotting and exile to become Queen Mary's archbishop of Canterbury.

After Mary's death in 1558 the crown went to Henry's only surviving child, Anne Boleyn's daughter Elizabeth, who turned out to have inherited many of her father's best qualities — intelligence, energy, resolution, boldness. Queen Elizabeth continued and extended the Tudor brand of powerful kingship. During her 45-year reign, she concerned herself mainly with England, avoiding the ancient dream of French conquest. Nevertheless, her subtle foreign policy strengthened English prestige, and "Good Queen Bess" is revered as one of England's greatest monarchs.

Henry VIII has been seen as a larger-than-life figure, a caricature of the avaricious tyrant, a fat, greedy pursuer of conquest, women, riches, and power who executed those who would thwart his desires. The reality is more complex. When Henry took the throne in 1509, the terrible upheaval of the Wars of the Roses was still fresh in his subjects' minds. His intelligence and vitality were welcomed by an England eager for a strong ruler. His decision to dissolve his marriage to Catherine of Aragon, while the first significant indication of the unappeasable willfulness that would corrupt his reign, must also be seen in the light of the dynastic struggles that had preceded his birth. There is little doubt that Henry, blessed with the luminous intelligence that had captivated such learned scholars as Erasmus and Thomas More, appreciated the importance of leaving a male heir whose legitimacy could not be questioned, and that consideration played no small part in his decision to marry Anne Boleyn and defy the papacy.

However, Henry's gifts were easily corrupted. As a young king he showed little concern for the dirty

Anne Askew, the first great Protestant martyr of England, and three companions are burned as heretics. Askew, who had enjoyed Queen Catherine's favor, repudiated the doctrine of transubstantiation held by the Catholic church.

work of government, preferring to leave those duties to the more than able Wolsey while he hunted and rode. Having then destroyed Wolsey and thrown aside the universal faith of his youth to marry Anne, there was nothing and no one to contain him. He squandered the national treasury in a series of fruitless wars and was consistently misled and duped by his European counterparts, Francis I of France and Charles V of the Holy Roman Empire. In order to finance his foreign adventures, he overtaxed his subjects and looted the countries' monasteries, provoking outright rebellion. As he grew increasingly

Despite his personal tragedies and a flawed foreign policy, Henry VIII left a monumental domestic legacy. He founded the Anglican church, and by strengthening Parliament's authority and expanding its role he laid the foundation for the modern state of England.

E. RONJAT

tyrannical, those who opposed him, even those who did not please him, were executed.

Despite the destructive aspects of his reign, Henry strengthened the power of the monarchy, which was no longer subject to the authority of the pope. Parliament was also made stronger by Henry's use of it to confirm his break with Rome and the line of his succession. Most important, England was free of the civil strife represented by the wars between the Yorks and Lancasters. Henry's heirs succeeded to the throne with little opposition. Given his obsession with having a son, it is ironic that it was his daughter Elizabeth who reigned over the flowering of English prosperity, culture, and power that became known as the Elizabethan Age.

Queen Mary enters London followed by her sister, Princess Elizabeth, in 1553. Mary reversed Henry's religious policies, persecuting Protestants so relentlessly that she was called "Bloody Mary."

Further Reading

Bush, Catherine. *Elizabeth I.* New York: Chelsea House, 1985.

Erickson, Carolly. *Great Harry.* New York: Summit, 1980.

Lacey, Robert. *The Life and Times of Henry VIII.* London: Weidenfeld and Nicolson, 1972.

Mattingly, Garrett. *Catherine of Aragon.* Boston: Little, Brown, 1941.

Ridley, Jasper. *Henry VIII.* New York: Viking, 1984.

Scarisbrick, J. J. *Henry VIII.* Berkeley: University of California, 1968.

Williams, Neville. *Henry VIII and His Court.* New York: Macmillan, 1972.

Chronology

June 28, 1491	Born Henry Tudor, second son of King Henry VII and Elizabeth of York
April 1509	Henry VII dies; Prince Henry accedes to the throne as Henry VIII
June 1509	Marries Catherine of Aragon
1513	Campaigns against the French; wins Battle of the Spurs
1515	Thomas Cardinal Wolsey appointed chancellor
Feb. 18, 1516	Princess Mary (Mary I) born
June 1520	Henry meets with Francis I of France at the Field of Cloth of Gold
1523	English invasion of France fails
June 1525	The Amicable Grant, a tax to support the war in France, provokes widespread rebellion
May 1529	Divorce trial of Henry and Catherine begins
Nov. 1529	Henry calls Reformation Parliament
1530	Wolsey dies en route to treason trial; Thomas More becomes chancellor; Thomas Cromwell enters Henry's service
1530–32	Henry asserts control over the English church
Jan. 25, 1533	Secretly marries Anne Boleyn
May–June 1533	Henry's marriage to Catherine declared invalid; Anne Boleyn is crowned queen
Sept. 7, 1533	Princess Elizabeth (Elizabeth I) born to Henry and Anne
Nov. 1534	Act of Supremacy declares Henry Supreme Head of the English church
1535	John Fisher and Thomas More executed for refusing to recognize royal supremacy in church matters
1536–39	Cromwell oversees dissolution of the monasteries
May 1536	Anne Boleyn beheaded for adultery; Henry marries Jane Seymour
1537	Pilgrimage of Grace rebellion suppressed
Oct. 12, 1537	Prince Edward (Edward VI) born to Henry and Jane Seymour; Jane dies two weeks later
1539	Act of Six Articles establishes the basic principles of the Anglican church
Jan. 1540	Henry marries Anne of Cleves
July 1540	Divorces Anne of Cleves; marries Catherine Howard; Cromwell executed
Feb. 1542	Catherine Howard beheaded for adultery
July 1543	Henry marries Catherine Parr
Jan. 28, 1547	Henry Tudor dies

Index

Frank Dwyer received his B.A. from New York University and his M.A. in English literature from the State University of New York at Buffalo. He has taught English literature at several New York-area schools, including Marymount College and the State University of New York at Buffalo. He worked as an actor and director in New York professional theater for 15 years. He is also the author of DANTON in the Chelsea House series WORLD LEADERS   PAST & PRESENT.

Arthur M. Schlesinger, jr., taught history at Harvard for many years and is currently Albert Schweitzer Professor of the Humanities at City University of New York. He is the author of numerous highly praised works in American history and has twice been awarded the Pulitzer Prize. He served in the White House as special assistant to Presidents Kennedy and Johnson.